READING THEORY NOW

READING THEORY NOW

An ABC of Good Reading with J. Hillis Miller

ÉAMONN DUNNE

Preface by J. Hillis Miller

and

Afterword by Julian Wolfreys

BLOOMSBURY

NEW YORK • LONDON • NEW DELHI • SYDNEY

Bloomsbury Academic

An imprint of Bloomsbury Publishing Plc

175 Fifth Avenue   50 Bedford Square
New York   London
NY 10010   WC1B 3DP
USA   UK

www.bloomsbury.com

First published 2013

Library of Congress Cataloging-in-Publication Data
Library of Congress Cataloging-in-Publication Data
Dunne, Éamonn, author.
Reading theory now: an ABC of good reading with J. Hillis
Miller/Éamonn Dunne.
pages cm.
Includes bibliographical references and index.
ISBN 978-1-4411-7458-1 (hardback) – ISBN 978-1-4411-1514-0 (paperback)
1. Miller, J. Hillis (Joseph Hillis), 1928–2. Criticism–United States. I. Title.
PS29.M55D88 2013
801'.95–dc23
2013000140

ISBN: HB: 978-1-4411-7458-1
PB: 978-1-4411-1514-0
ePDF: 978-1-4411-0842-5
ePub: 978-1-4411-9051-2

Typeset by Deanta Global Publishing Services, Chennai, India
Printed and bound in the United States of America

For Aidan and Ciarán

CONTENTS

PREFACE

Exergue: Miller from A to Z
Or:
Miller on Dunne on Miller

J. HILLIS MILLER

Éamonn Dunne has understood my writings extremely well, almost too well for comfort. This wonderfully witty, subtle, and perceptive little book is the best introduction I know to my work. It unzips Miller from A to Z. If you read *Reading Theory Now: An ABC of Good Reading with J. Hillis Miller*, you will hardly need actually to read Miller's work, unless you happen to want to do so. Of course I hope that will be the case, especially after you read this book. Dunne, by the way, in case you have any doubts, brilliantly glosses in the opening section, *Excursus, Excursus,* the meanings he gives to his title.

I give high marks to four features of *Reading Theory Now*:

A is for Acute. I have said Dunne's book is "witty." This is a way of describing the constant delight of just reading it. It is a "good read." One example of its wit is the title of the wonderfully-on-the-mark generalizing prefatory section, before he gets to abc. It is called "Excursus, Excursus." This, as the Excursus makes clear, is a play on "Excuses, Excuses," since the Excursus apologizes self-consciously for its strategies of condensation and organization. Dunne imagines a reader protesting by saying, disparagingly, "Excuses, excuses! Come on, get on with it." "Excursus, Excursus" may also be a somewhat covert reference to an essay of mine called "Promises, Promises." Dunne's "Excursus" promises that he will write a small book on my work with an entry for each letter of the alphabet, though of course the Excursus was written after the book, as a preposterous cart before the horse. Dunne's book is full of such ironic plays on words, as, for example, the innocent word "glossary" ("the following fragmented glossary of Millerian terminology") turns into the more threatening "critico-glossolalia," cited from Nicholas Royle. "Glossolalia" means "gift of tongues," as in Acts 2: 1–13, but also "fabricated nonmeaningful speech, especially as associated with certain schizophrenic syndromes" (*American Heritage Dictionary*). Take your choice.

B is for arBitrary. I admire the way Dunne makes clear that his book does not present a systematic account of "key terms in Miller's literary-critical matrix." It is just a series of reflections on some words I happen to have used and reused, words that are, Dunne claims, salient in my work. This arbitrary and disconnected ordering is of course made evident in the meaninglessness of giving one entry for each letter of the alphabet, from a to z. No reason whatsoever beyond whimsical ones can be given for that nonorderly ordering, though of course the model is those children's books that teach the alphabet: "A is for apple." This alphabetical choice forces Dunne to stretch things a bit, to think of words for "q" or "y." "Queer" and "yarn" are words not all that frequently used in my work, but the entries are fascinating (to me at least). They are brilliant evasions of their arbitrariness.

Dunne's word for "z" is of course "zero." He probably knows that I wrote my little book, *Zero Plus One*, in desperate response to a desperate request from my old friend Julian Wolfreys to write an entry for a book on critical terms he was putting together that was to have one entry for each letter of the alphabet. He emailed me beseechingly to say he did not have a "z," and could I write something in a hurry, perhaps on "zeugma." Somewhat perversely I turned down "zeugma," but said, as a complete shot in the dark, that I would try "zero." I found the history of zero fascinating and enigmatic, even as a critical term (*The Degree Zero of Writing*). My entry got longer and longer, until only a bit of it could be included in Wolfreys' book. The whole essay was published as a separate small book. Wolfreys' book, by the way, is called *glossalalia—an alphabet of keywords*. Note the stress on "a." It is not a mistake in spelling. Much more could and should be written about wordplay and puns in literary critical writing from Aristotle on. It is hard, even sometimes for Aristotle, that most serious and rational of philosophers, to be completely solemn in writing about literature. Dunne recognizes what has always been occasional, arbitrary, often commissioned, in my books and essays, but he might have made even more of that fortuitousness. A book falls into my hands. I read it. I then find myself wanting to teach it or to write something about it. I had no idea whether or not "zero" would lead anywhere. So, an alphabetical order is as good as any.

One way Dunne made his work easier was quite arbitrarily to focus especially on my four books stemming from the so-called Ariadne Project. This means his terms are drawn especially from books and essays in my "middle period," to give it a pompous name. Though I would not follow Wallace Stevens by saying "one's early things give one the creeps," nor, God forbid, follow the ageing Swift who said of his early work, *The Tale of a Tub,* "God, what a genius I had then!" nevertheless I view my earlier writings with some detachment, as almost having been written by someone else. I by no means, however, disown them. I wrote 'em, and I take responsibility for whatever may have happened when they were read by others. I am immensely, naively, flattered and pleased when someone somewhere in the world emails me to say, "I read one of your essays in a university course and it greatly influenced me." That makes my day.

If I were to gently challenge Éamonn Dunne's choices of words for a given letter, I'd say I'm more interested now in my most recent work. He chooses "character" for his "c," and weaves a wonderful arabesque around my old essay on that word. If I were to choose a "c-word" these days, however, I'd be more likely to pick "climate change," or even Tom Cohen's phrase "critical climate change," or "community," or "conflagration" (as in "HoloCaust"), or "circumlocution," or "computers," as in "computer games," or "connected," or "catachresis" (which Dunne discusses), or "catastrophe," as in "catastrophic health care costs" and "ecocatastrophe," or even "chaos." For "k" I might pick "Kafkesque," as a name for the nightmarish society we live in now. For "w" perhaps "why?" as in "Why read literature at all in these disquieting days of teletechnological innovation, globalization, financial meltdown, melting polar ice, and rising sea levels?" How can literature survive the internet and the irresistible allure of online video games? As Captain Boyle in Sean O'Casey's *Juno and the Paycock* says, "Th' whole worl's in a terrible state o' chassis." (It is a symptom of how computers and the internet have changed everything, even literary study, that I was able to verify my citation from O'Casey in a few moments by Googling "state of chassis," which led me to the Wikipedia entry for the play that includes the citation [http://en.wikipedia.org/wiki/Juno_and_the_Paycock. Accessed December 17, 2011.]) These days of chassis hardly seem the time to worry about the minutiae of narrative theory or about fine tropological distinctions, as the water rises up to our chins, and storms become ever more severe.

I cite these alternative possible words (and therefore worlds) not to disqualify the importance in my work of any of the words Dunne chooses. I want rather to indicate that the new concerns of my most recent work suggest how easy it would be to get a different result by choosing a different set of words from a to z and then following out their roles in what I have written. Dunne admits this arbitrariness in his "Excursus, Excursus." If my works are viewed panoramically, synchronically, all at once, as rows of books and essays on the shelf, no doubt a concern for narrative lines and for the theory of tropes looms large, as it does for Éamonn Dunne as a reader of my writing. From my own perspective, however, my publications are part of an ongoing, ever-changing project, with earlier works fading off into the past. What I have recently written is, naturally, of greatest interest to me, including things not yet published (like this present text which I am now sitting at my computer composing). Éamonn Dunne has no reason to know my unpublished works, or works in progress, or plans for future writings.

C is for Comparison and Contrast. One of the greatest values of *Reading Theory Now* is the way it constantly juxtaposes my work with citations from Sigmund Freud, Jacques Derrida, Nicholas Royle, Paul de Man, Jean-Luc Nancy, Maurice Blanchot, Friedrich Nietzsche, Geoffrey Bennington, Derek Attridge, and many other theorists. These authoritative comparisons give Dunne's book a richness and depth that greatly add to its utility for readers.

D is for Diversion. One of the strongest aspects of *Reading Theory Now* is Dunne's citation and discussion of works my work makes him think of but which I did not happen to "treat." This is a feature of his earlier big book on my work that I greatly admire. Dunne does not just paraphrase my writing. He turns aside to quote and to make brilliant comments on poems by Siegfried Sassoon and by Yeats, on the "Choose Your Own Adventure" series of children's books, on Shakespeare's *A Midsummer Night's Dream*, on Wilde's preface to *The Picture of Dorian Gray*, on Dickens' *David Copperfield*, on D. H. Lawrence's *Women in Love*, on Beckett's *Waiting for Godot*, on Hemingway's "A Clean, Well-Lighted Place," on Nabokov's *Lolita*, on Flann O'Brien's *At Swim-Two-Birds*, on Paul Auster's "City of Glass," and, perhaps best of all, on Melville's *Moby Dick* and *Billy Budd*. These constant detours away from the strict Miller line are arguably the best parts of Dunne's book. At any rate they have given me the most pleasure. Even when discussing my readings, he brilliantly goes beyond what I have said, as in his remarks about Henchard kissing the Bible in Hardy's *The Mayor of Casterbridge*. What greater success can a critic have than to instigate her or his readers to go forth and do likewise/otherwise.

I could easily continue through the rest of the alphabet, from e to z, identifying other aspects of Éamonn Dunne's book that I much like. It is high time, however, for me to vanish and to let you get on with reading the book proper, not just this parergon or exergue. Please excuse me for this over-long excursus. "Out of the abundance of the heart the mouth speaketh" (Matthew 12: 34). I am confident my heartfelt gratitude to Éamonn Dunne is an abundance of that sort.

Sedgwick, Maine/Deer Isle, Maine

December 17, 2011/October 26, 2012

INTRODUCTION

Excursus, Excursus

Writing in reserve: a hydrapoetics or critico-glossolalia.
As simple as abc.

NICHOLAS ROYLE, *After Derrida*

If things were simple, word would have gotten around,
as you say in English.

JACQUES DERRIDA, *Limited Inc*

Translations

Beginning with that kind of speech act called an excuse I feel I must
provide some reasons for the following fragmented glossary of
Millerian terminology, in however tentative or furtive a fashion. We
are on slippery ground here, and I am only too aware of it. Any list-
like rendering of recurring topics in J. Hillis Miller's work is bound
by that very procedure to be exclusive and somewhat arbitrary. One
cannot catalogue or assimilate the singular usage of each particular
term followed up here by a simple process of grafting—taking a
particular usage and applying a theoretical apparatus or structure—
without also inadvertently performing some violent sundering. Each

individual term below is also, with the exception of a handful of neologisms invented for a specific occasion, context-bound, hewed from a reading of a particular author's work and given life as a glimpse of the act of reading in its inventive and surprising acknowledgment of the unique richness of each literary work explored.

Our opening term, for instance, comes by way of Miller's reading of Proust, where the term is used by Marcel to describe a certain situation within that novel, but even Marcel acknowledges that he has taken it from the "rhetoricians." Miller's dehiscent or somewhat anasemical re-imagining of this term can only really be made sense of in terms of that reading. Like so-called Derridean terms such as "hymen," or "pharmakon," each one is invariably adopted from the work being read; the tendency with Miller's work is to elaborate on something already there at work in the text. Each act of reading is a performative action, a *finding* of what was there already, a local oddness or peculiarity too easily passed over and forgotten by a hasty reading. Other terms such as "beginnings" and "middles" are opportunities to be more conscientious about what we post-Aristotelians normally take for granted in any given text, a chance to catch a glimpse of the utter strangeness of literary works. Indeed, this is the one fundamental point I will offer about the "strategy" Miller employs in his acts of reading—a search for meaning in the most bizarre and esoteric moments in literary works which have somehow been accepted as canonical. This would seem to have been the closest thing to a guiding motivation in all of his criticism. As he put it to Robert Moynihan in 1982, "to some degree, it is still my motivation as a critic to 'translate'. When I get riled up about attacks of the sort we are talking about [he means Gerald Graff's attack on his writings in *Literature Against Itself*], I recall that most people in literature just don't realize how very strange the works of literature are. I still feel that. I'm still fascinated by that. If you just look at the works of literature in the most open and naïve way, they are just very peculiar. They are like Southern California" (Moynihan 1986, 111). The point is reiterated in a later interview with Julian Wolfreys in 2004, where he stresses his "double" interest in the peculiarity and oddness of literary language and his "scientific" tendency to account for it in some way. Here, he also rather jocosely, perhaps even scientifically, professes "Miller's law": "The greatest critics are those whose readings exceed their theoretical presuppositions" (Wolfreys 2005, 414). And in a sense this excess of reading is the undoing of this very project, if it tries to account for Miller's work, *and* also its chance to actually do something with the words already there in a performative gesture of proximity and distance, discovery and invention, interpretation and reading.

In what follows and, in many ways what I have said at more length in my longer book on Miller, *J. Hillis Miller and the Possibilities of Reading*, the general assumption is that each act of reading is in some way always *sui generis*, singular, original, however strong the tendency to account for it by placing it in a tradition or under the banner of some assumed theoretical enterprise. Each act of reading in this short introductory book has faced a double bind, or "blind" as Miller might have it: read Miller reading or read then reread Miller. To remain faithful or responsible to Miller's work is paradoxically and at the same time to express the most violent irresponsibility. By this I mean that I have not been seeking a universal ground for acts of reading in Miller's work, one would have to be very single-minded or stubborn to do so; nor have I been attempting to forge a biographico-theoretical rendering of his entire oeuvre, where movements between schools can be shown to have influenced and directed his work. No doubt this is to a large extent the actual case as it is with any critic and as can be shown with the early influence of Kenneth Burke (his PhD thesis on Dickens in 1952), Georges Poulet (his first three books), Paul De Man and Jacques Derrida (for the "ethical turn" and the later work) on his writing career. But what most interests me in this volume, and what has most interested me about Miller's work over the years, is this attention to the *event* and *act* of reading, that law which states that literary works have an uncanny way of escaping cognition and will, given half a chance, always exceed a reader's expectations. A cursory glance at Miller's prefaces and introductions will confirm this. One paradigmatic example of which are the opening pages of *Fiction and Repetition*: "this book is not a work of theory as such, but a series of readings of important nineteenth- and twentieth-century English novels . . . The focus of my readings is on the 'how' of readings rather than on its 'what'. . . . I try to attend to the threads of the tapestry of words in each case rather than simply to the picture the novel makes when viewed from a distance" (FR, 3).

This critico-glossolalia will, therefore, not serve as an account of key terms in an assumed literary-critical matrix so much as an initial, provisional, even speculative foray into the working of the works themselves, with specific interest in the four books stemming from the so-called Ariadne Project, which Miller details as a result of a notebook entry in his journal on January 4, 1976.[1] The result, that is, of a promise to follow Ariadne's thread through the many-chambered labyrinth called narrative.

This will also have been my excuse for an excursus. No doubt it will be perverse. Indeed, the funny thing about excuses is that they are always perverse. Once you make an excuse it always doubles or trebles or quadruples in an incessantly productive series of attempted exonerations. Excuses in other words generate storytelling. They keep the storylines from ever reaching their goals. Which is one reason why, as Derrida puts it in "Circumfession," "one always asks for pardon when one writes" (Derrida 1993, 46).[2] Or like Socrates in the *Protagoras,* when in excusing himself for being tardy to a meeting with a friend, he generates almost the entire narrative: "As for the Marlow of *Heart of Darkness* and the Quentin of Faulkner's *Absalom, Absalom!,* so for Socrates here storytelling is a form of exculpation. It is a form, however, in which one story generates another and that another, as if the excuse could never quite get itself performed for certain. . . . One story fathers another in a never-ending but unsuccessful search for the foundational story that will have paternal authority over all the others and give the excuser grounds for his excuse. If that were to happen, the relation of fathering would reverse in an encounter with the father of all stories" (T, 62). The more conscientious the excuser, the more the storylines will proliferate. Each excuse begins again the attempt to bring the narrative back to a paterno-logo-centric originary moment only to show that that moment has wandered off.

Not entitled

As we will see below, titles are promises that can never be kept. They are never, if you think about it conscientiously, fully realizable in the texts that follow them. Titles, in this sense, are always somewhat provisional, abrupt authorial decisions that herald nothing less than passages into unknown vistas, vistas which always to some degree or other challenge the premise that has led into them. If you take a moment to look at some of the titles of J. Hillis Miller's books for example, you might begin to see a challenge to readers to intuit why and how titles are often undermining received assumptions about what you will find in these books.

Speech Acts in Literature sounds as if it is as straightforward a title as you are likely to encounter. The book is after all about speech act theory and its influence on critical thinking about literature. It is certainly easily identifiable in this category because each of its chapters predictably discusses a major figure in the field. For instance, the book opens with an introduction to J. L. Austin, the father of the discipline, and the inaugural document of that school *How to Do Things with Words*. Offering clear and concise discussions of key moments in Austinian thinking, it then progresses to discussions of Derrida's writings, which invigorates and challenges Austin's work while simultaneously criticizing its heir apparent, John Searle. A further chapter discusses the profound effects speech act theory has had on Paul de Man's works from as early as 1975. The book's last two chapters, one on Wittgenstein and one on Proust, explicitly interrogate these redoubtable philosophical musings for their practical powers in reading literature and literary theory.

So, why do we need to worry about the title? For one thing that title goes two ways at once. Primarily, it states an explicit agenda to discuss the "theory" of speech acts and how that theory works in literature. As I've just said, it meets that challenge by doing exactly what it says it's going to do. On the other hand, the title can also be read as a performative statement whereby the words "do" something rather than simply describe a state of affairs. Read latterly, the title is a kind of exclamation: watch out for this! It states that speech *acts* in literature, those words have power, a power that doesn't always chime with sturdy epistemological measures. Reading a novel, that is, is not quite the same as reading a dry linguistic philosophical discussion about how words actually function grammatically or syntactically in a given sentence or passage or context. Reported speech in literary texts has itself an uncanny and inaugural power to bring something new into the world. Speech acts in novels act in ways that are never fully verifiable, saturable, or containable in any given context. Promises, declarations, pardons, lies, and excuses have all power to disrupt our lives inside and outside of the virtual space-time of novels. The "in literature" of the title can be read ironically, therefore, to suggest the ways in which speech acts in our everyday world and speech acts in literary texts are not all that easily distinguishable. That "in literature" does not guarantee that the speech act will not in some way be felicitous or have purchase in the real world, in the here and now.

Dreaming impossibly

Reading Theory Now is likewise a title that comes to me as a necessity, a strategy and an adventure. Each of my three words sits beside its partner and invites the reader to think of the connection between them. What could be more innocent and straightforward? You are now reading a book about theory. Specifically, you are reading a glossary of terms that come by way of my readings of literary theory, terms suggested to me by my readings of the author-scholar-reader-theorist J. Hillis Miller. But what happens when theories are read? What happens in the event of reading or rereading theory in the here and now?

I give three reasons why I take this title and why I feel these words harbor a kind of implicit magnetic field that by turns polarizes and attracts the other words in my title. These tensions merit some explaining:

1) Reading: What does it mean to read well? What does it mean to be a good reader? If you are looking at this page presumably you can read already, so you may be wondering why I feel the need to explain this term to you. Some readers might even have found this last statement a little patronizing and have by now decided to read something else entirely. The question reminds me of a dismissive outburst I overheard a young college student intone at the literary theory section of a small bookshop in Williamsburg, Virginia some years ago. "Literary theory," said the student, "Ha! How to read a book." The assumption, I take it, was that the neatly ordered columns of books available under the exclusive heading "literary theory" suggested to him that those books were generic primers designed to provide a catch-all framework for readers to use on any book they may happen upon in future: the Marxist reading, the Feminist reading, the Structuralist reading, the Poststructuralist reading, and so on. My presumption is that he saw in those books a strangely paradoxical gesture to stop reading, to have finished with it. The sentiment resonates with a passage in Derrida's *The Post Card*. There Derrida, criticizing the hasty reader, says the following:

Because I still like him, I can foresee the impatience of the *bad* reader: this is the way I name or accuse the fearful reader, the reader in a hurry to be determined, decided upon deciding (in order to annul, in other words to bring back to oneself, one has to wish to know in advance what to expect, one wishes to expect (oneself)). Now, it is bad, and I know no other definition of the bad, it is bad to predestine one's reading, it is always bad to foretell. It is bad, reader, no longer to like retracing one's steps" (Derrida 1987, 4).

For Miller, likewise, reading should be governed by the expectation of surprise; it ought to open itself up to the singular event of the new, open itself in Derrida's words to the coming of the other (VP, 33). Good reading is marked by a hospitality to the impossible arrival of the wholly other, to a heterogeneity and polyvocality that exceeds the cold comfort of hermeneutical finality; it is, therefore, left to wander. If reading is predestined, directed, goal-oriented, and prejudicial, then it is not reading. Good reading in the Millerian universe means slow reading (OL, 122). It means taking one's time over the text. It means intense labor, working through, sifting out, peering into and being guided by those words there on the page, not some prefabricated theoretical framework that acts like a pattern on a laminate that may be laid over the text in order to pinpoint the meaning of the text. Good reading goes on, impossibly, knowing that the reading will never be done, that it is always the desperation of a bet against knowing for sure what an objective knowledge of the text might be (LM, 26). This is why reading cannot, as I've argued elsewhere, be taught.[3] It is also why reading Miller engages you in an act of reading that simultaneously, self-reflexively, brings that act of reading into the foreground. "We struggle to read from the moment we wake in the morning until the moment we fall asleep at night, and what are our dreams but more lessons in the pain of the impossibility of reading, or rather the pain of having no way whatsoever of knowing whether or not we may have in our discursive wanderings and aberrancies stumbled by accident on the right reading" (ER, 59).

As soon as we move from the "what" of textual analysis to the "how" of textual analysis, we are in the exorbitant realm of the reader. That "how" is not prescriptive, rather it is indicative of a recurring failure that may or may not get better; it indicates a knowledge that reading is perpetually peripatetic, perverse, perambulatory, and never ever even present to itself. There are no guarantees for the good reader, never any ways of knowing that one is even becoming a good reader. There are only ever new beginnings, as if we were Sisyphus-like learning to read all over again each day. "To live is to read" (ER, 59). The end of reading is death, the hidden ground of all speech acts (LC, 223).

2) Theory: Theory and reading, says Miller in an important statement on this issue, are "asymmetrical" (TNT, vii; VP, 95; T, 323). In one sense, close, rhetorical reading is the undoing or ruination of theoretical premonition, especially in the etymological sense of the word "theory" as a clear seeing or seeing through. It would surely be more apt to say that the closer one reads, the more time one takes with one's own reading, the more one sees the difficulties of that clear seeing and the impossibility of generalized theoretical categorization. The more one reads the more one notices the possibilities of other readings, competing readings, readings that undo the salutary certainty of predestination. Good reading teaches one to unlearn one's habits of reading, to see again, anew, even in the texts we feel we know. Reading theory in this way alerts us to the way that theoretical texts themselves must be read as scrupulously and rhetorically as literary texts. If we are responsive to or responsible in our readings, we will come to see that theory is not the end of reading, but its beginning.

Theories are provisional; they help us get on with our readings, but they can never bring fully into the light the mellifluous complexities of reading. "We need theory now and then," says Miller in his book of that name, "to help us get on with the serious business of reading. If each performative speech act is unique, for just this time, place, and occasion only, so a work of theory, insofar as it is performative, is oriented toward its own time and place. It is what is needed now and then, not for all time, to make reading possible" (TNT, vii).

Consequently, the fact that theories are repeatable, programmable, and iterable means that there is no escaping theory either, hence the asymmetry between them. Saying that any reading is unique in the time of its performance, in its situation and context is a theoretical proposition through and through; it is a generalizing expression for the activity of reading itself. Though reading changes and challenges theory, and however much it undoes it, it is never finished with it. To put this another way, "there is no reading that is not theoretical, but the actual act of reading is always to some degree the disconfirmation of theory" (VP, 94). This is of course as true for my readings in what follows as it is for any readings J. Hillis Miller performs in his own work. The closer you get to seeing how this happens in your own reading the further away, paradoxically, you get from any consensus about the activity of reading and its relationship with theoretical models. This whirligig may be maddening, chaotic, and scandalous, but it signals a resistance, as Paul de Man noticed long ago, that is central to theory, namely that the language of theory is the language of "self-resistance" (de Man 1986, 19). There is a sense, therefore, and however counterintuitive it may seem, that J. Hillis Miller is not a literary theorist. He is not a literary theorist if by that term we assume a predilection for prediction in the course of a given reading. Nor is he a literary theorist in the sense that the young student in the bookshop presumed that theory meant teaching a generic reading strategy. You will not find one in Miller and I have not sought to provide one here. Miller argues forcefully in the concluding pages of *Topographies* that "to translate theory is to traduce it, to betray it" (T, 319). He does not mean by this that it *cannot* happen, that theoretical writings are not being translated from one language or culture to another all the time. It is pellucidly clear that theory does indeed travel from place to place, country to country, and culture to culture every day. What is not clear are the effects that this traveling has on those theories. That theory is indeed translatable, excessively, promiscuously so means that it is an intrinsic effect of theoretical speculation that it never hits its mark. "A theoretical formulation never quite adequately expresses the insight that comes from reading" (T, 336). Or, as Barbara Johnson had it in *The Critical Difference* "it is precisely the way theory misses its target that produces incalculable and interesting effects elsewhere" (Johnson 1985, xii).

3) *Now*: I take it that Johnson's use of the word "elsewhere" in my previous citation alludes also to another time, the time of another reading, another context and situation. Missing the mark in that reading alludes to the performative power of theory to shake up,

reinvigorate, and alter perceptions. It also emphasizes the time of theory, its provisional nature. Theories are time-bound. They take place in a particular time and place and are bound to that time and place in a way that a reading is not (TNT, vii). Reading I. A. Richards' theoretical assumptions in *Practical Criticism*, for example, seems extremely dated now, tied to a certain Cambridge cultural capital of the 1920s. Though the readings themselves are still of much interest to readers today, few of us would believe that Richards' methodological strategies are unproblematic.

The word "now," in an ageing Irish parlance, is often used as a filler. Like the French word "alors," it acts as a temporary punctuation in speech, a sort of placeholder for "so," "okay," and as a slightly younger generation would say nowadays, "like." "Now" in colloquial Irish speech is strangely used to put off or even displace that now of communication, to continue going on, if you like, like Beckett's lines from *The Unnamable*: "Where now? Who now? When now?" (Beckett 2006, 285). It is not uncommon either to hear someone say "There you are now," as a kind of salutation or greeting expressing fondness or camaraderie. Linguists would call this a form of phatic speech—an expression used for social rather than for communicative purposes. To which we might also imagine Beckett's Estragon from *Waiting for Godot* ironically respond: "Am I?"[4] The repetitions of "now" in Beckett operate like Derrida's wonderful sentence in "Différance" that repeats the word "presence" in order to emphasize the trace-effect of différance (difference and deferral) at issue throughout that seminal essay:

> An interval must separate the **present** from what it is not in order
> for the **present** to be itself, but this interval that constitutes it as

present must, by the same token, divide the **present** in and of itself, thereby also dividing, along with the **present**, everything that is thought on the basis of the **present**, that is, in our metaphysical language, every being, and singularly substance or the subject (Derrida 1986a, 13) [my emphases].

These six "presences" in a single sentence undermine the sense of the sentence and the sense that presence is ever present in and of itself, in the here and now. There is never a single moment full stop, not one, nor has there ever been one—one that is not already divided into two, three, four, and so on. Now. There you are. So no now, not ever, nor has there ever been a now, nor will there ever be a now.

So in one sense, in the present sense, the now of reading theory is impossible. It can never be, since it is "riven by difference in the present . . . the constant invention and intervention of something wholly other" (Ill, 56). Nevertheless, the now of this title signifies that the time of reading is also what is important for me in what follows. Each act of reading came about in a particular time and in a particular place. Each letter suggested itself to me within my readings of particular works (literary or theoretical) and they act, therefore, to remind me of their happenings, as events that seem to me now as fresh as they were in that singular moment of their arrival.

For J. Hillis Miller, what happens when he reads draws him to moments in literature that are extremely odd and require some explaining. Following him down these paths is no easy task, since it means you have to go back to the original text he reads in order to see why and how these aporias and paradoxes occur. It is not enough to read Miller reading. You have to go back to the texts themselves.

I have, in all good conscience, traveled back as far as possible and as often as possible to those texts to see why Miller has said such extraordinarily strange things about them. The results of those readings can be encountered in my longer book on Miller. In this work, I have tried to follow a much different path. Here, I have been led by my own readings of Miller, James, Blanchot, Freud, Melville, and de Man, among others, to new texts, texts I have encountered for myself. I have endeavored to follow a call those other works have made on me personally. I have tried to account for that call in my own readings and in my own time. I don't for a moment believe that this work has been an attempt to apply Miller, Derrida, de Man, or whoever else falls under that fraught rubric "theorist." Rather the gesture has always been to something other, to a vocation for reading I feel obliged to follow, from where and to whom I know not.

Who now? What now? Why now? Being responsible to reading has meant, in a way being irresponsible to theory, countersigning in the name of reading what has gone before. To read well, I believe, is to struggle with theory's grip, to write from the heart as well as the head, and to follow as far as possible the rhythms of one's own thinking while knowing all the while that every reading is motivated. I don't believe that there can ever be an escape from theory; I don't believe there is a neutral position. But I emphasize the reading in my title and stake all on the desire to open the text to a new beginning, to come close to those moments when reading happens regardless of want, where what happens just happens. My only strategy has been to say what I wanted to say about a particular word and a particular text at a given time and then to stop. I have said what I wanted to say and leave it to the reader to go on, impossibly, reading theory now.

Notes

1 See the preface to *Ariadne's Thread* where Miller explains the birth of this project out of the introduction to *Fiction and Repetition* and the subsequent plans he initially made for the project which eventually became: *Ariadne's Thread* (1992), *Illustration* (1992), *Topographies* (1994), and *Reading Narrative* (1999). In the preface to the latter, Miller suggests that *Fiction and Repetition* (1982) should be seen alongside these works as the result of a promise he made to himself to tease out the ideas suggested to him while writing the introduction to that early work. With this in mind, the glossary that follows here pays particular attention to these works.

2 What is interesting in Derrida's sentence, by the way, is that it appears as a quotation in "Circumfession" which Derrida then links to another fragmented narrative, namely, "The Post Card." Once the excuse is made that is, the storyline immediately doubles.

3 See the concluding chapter of my *J. Hillis Miller and the Possibilities of Reading* (New York: Continuum, 2010), pp. 117–122.

4 "So there you are again," says Vladimir in the opening lines of *Waiting for Godot*. To which Estragon replies with hilarious philosophical whimsicality "Am I?" Miller also, by the way, devotes several pages to this phrase in a reading of Henry James' *The Wings of the Dove* (where it appears quite often) in *Literature as Conduct*, pp. 193–197: "Of each 'There you are' it can be said that it marks an event that cuts the person put there by it off from what came before." Estragon is a *Dasein*, a being there, as Heidegger's idiom would have it, bound to that temporalization that both subdivides and anchors subjectivity at once. Beckett's "So there you are again" is yet another form of this colloquial expression. The comedy comes from knowing that the phrase is an idiomatic Irish greeting as well as an existential question. The latter never realized until someone like Estragon challenges it. The "again" that concludes the statement is echoed in the following lines by Estragon's irritable "Not now, not now" which emphasizes further the difficulty with the phrase.

ACKNOWLEDGMENTS

I owe an enormous debt of gratitude to a great many people whose ideas and support, whether they have known this or not, have been continually inspiring and productive for me. I thank the IRCHSS and Graham Allen, Martin McQuillan, Jonathan Mitchell, Graham Price and Nicholas Royle for their lively discussions and commentaries at a conference on the work of J. Hillis Miller held in Dublin in June, 2012; Arthur Bradley and John Schad were also instrumental in helping this happen. To Dragan Kujundžić I give thanks for not only introducing his film, *The First Sail: J. Hillis Miller*, at the event but also for his indefatigable goodwill and unending generosity. J. Hillis Miller and Julian Wolfreys have helped me with this project from its earliest stages and I offer my deepest gratitude to them for astute observations and incomparable learning in all things literary and theoretical. An earlier version of my reading of Paul Auster was presented at a conference on the ethics of fiction at the University of Zaragoza, Spain and subsequently appeared in an edited collection entitled *On the Turn*, edited by Bàrbara Arizti and Silvia Martínez-Falquina; I thank them for allowing me to reproduce some of this material here. I am grateful also to Arthur Broomfield, Donal Evoy, Terence Augustine Halpin, Haaris Naqvi, Mark Quinn, Kathy Reilly and Seán Ó Súilleabháin for helping me think through important issues along the way. I give special thanks to my good friend and teacher Michael O'Rourke. Finally, for their constant goodwill and encouragement I thank my wife Jenny and our three boys, Peter, Aidan and Ciarán.

ABBREVIATIONS OF WORKS BY J. HILLIS MILLER

AT   *Ariadne's Thread: Story Lines* (New Haven: Yale University Press, 1992).

BH   *Black Holes* (Stanford: Stanford University Press, 1999).

CC   *The Conflagration of Community: Fiction Before and After Auschwitz* (Chicago: University of Chicago Press, 2011).

DG   *The Disappearance of God: Five Nineteenth-Century Writers* (Cambridge: Harvard University Press, 1963).

ER   *The Ethics of Reading* (New York: Columbia University Press, 1987).

FD   *For Derrida* (New York: Fordham University Press, 2009).

FR   *Fiction and Repetition: Seven English Novels* (Cambridge: Harvard University Press, 1982).

HH   *Hawthorne and History: Defacing It* (Oxford: Basil Blackwell, 1991).

IL   *Illustration* (Cambridge: Harvard University Press, 1992).

LC   *Literature as Conduct: Speech Acts in Henry James* (New York: Fordham UP, 2005).

LM   *The Linguistic Moment: From Wordsworth to Stevens* (Princeton: Princeton University Press, 1985).

ON *On Literature* (London: Routledge, 2002).

O *Others* (Princeton: Princeton UP, 2001).

PR *Poets of Reality: Six Twentieth-Century Writers* (Cambridge: Harvard University Press, 1966).

RN *Reading Narrative* (Norman: University of Oklahoma Press, 1999).

RT *Reading for Our Time:* Adam Bede *and* Middlemarch *Revisited* (Edinburgh: Edinburgh University Press, 2012).

SA *Speech Acts in Literature* (Stanford: Stanford University Press, 2001).

T *Topographies* (Stanford: Stanford University Press, 1995).

TNT *Theory Now and Then* (London: Harvester Wheatsheaf, 1991).

TPP *Tropes, Parables, Performatives* (London: Harvester Wheatsheaf, 1991).

VP *Versions of Pygmalion* (Cambridge: Harvard University Press, 1990).

Z *Zero plus One* (València: Universitat de València, 2003).

A before B—of course...

a

"Anacoluthon doubles the story line and so makes the story probably a lie" (RN, 149). It expresses the impossibility of following the line from beginning to end, the impossibility of tracing any narrative thread from its origins to its completion without some kind of illicit wandering, that is, without becoming irresponsible or irresponsive (in whatever degree) to the demands made on us by the text. This of course applies to any story, including this one. The word also signifies the problematic of a response to the promise of the logos, therefore actually necessitating the lie. One could perhaps reiterate the idea by saying that storylines are assembled and dismembered by the implicit demand made on each reader to remember the way at all times, to follow the line back and forth from the clue (the word means the ball of thread from which the line is drawn) to the center of the labyrinth, "some triumphant Q.E.D" (AT, xii).

There is of course also something here in the clue itself that shares in the complexity of the narrative line, since the "clue" is another line, perhaps even more labyrinthine than the labyrinth, merely waiting to be unraveled. The clue as origin of the line is itself a labyrinth of labyrinths, a repetition of the problematic, just as the "I" is the promise of the logos and its undoing, the very (im)possibility of the story line. "'I' promise to tell the whole truth" is a performative speech act; it functions as a felicitous act which does not depend on the self-identical nature of the "I," an impossibility, but rather on the *memory* of the "I" that posits. Promises are then always subject to yet more promises which cannot be known beforehand, promises are infinitely differed, great Nietzschean yea-sayings. They depend on the future, on the "super-monster of eventness," the *à-venir*, as Derrida would have it. As such, like the narrative line, they imply an ethics as a kind of Socratic anamnesis, a remembrance which is somehow both knowable and nonknowable.

The line is a repetition of something that went before and will come again, in the sense that letters are lines whose differential curvatures separate and distinguish them from other letters. They are repetitions of a certain figure or figures. But they are also inaugural inscriptions to whatever infinitesimally minor or inconsequential degree. Each line figures (draws, weaves, patterns, quilts, represents, recites) a way and a wandering at the level of the letter and of the narrative: "The intelligibility of writing depends on this twisting and breaking of the line that interrupts or confounds its linearity and opens up the possibility of repeating that segment, while at the same time preventing any closure of its meaning" (AT, 8). The line, therefore, in an uncanny manner, depends on the possibility and impossibility of its function as a straight line: its possibility is dependent on its function as an approximation of its own ideal figuration, in the very same way that the letter of the text implies its ability to be identical to its forebears and different simultaneously. Lines are only linear because of their differences from other lines. They are only lines precisely because of their iterability within (or without) that system of differences; one doesn't, for instance, ordinarily think of two parallel lines as the same line. Zeno's paradoxes and Heraclitus' philosophical fragments have expressed these sentiments for millennia, and can be shown to be at odds with the dominant presuppositions of the logocentric Western tradition, as Nietzsche's eternal recurrence has also shown: "The line, Ariadne's thread, is both the labyrinth and a means of safely retracing the labyrinth. The thread and the maze are each the origin of which the other is a copy, or each is a copy that makes the other, already there, an origin: Ich bin dein Labyrinth" (AT, 16).

The anacoluthon is an abrupt breach in the line, as when in Proust's *recherche* Albertine shifts pronouns intermittently in mid-sentence, an agrammatically insinuating force breaking through the sequentiality of the narrative line and alerting us to the structurality or fabricated nature of all narratives. It makes the line a lie or nonsequitur. And it shows that the possibility of storytelling finds its grounds at the trembling limits of recollection and prevarication. Indeed, "it's a fact that, like the self-identity of the subject, memory *is* or rather *must*, *should* be an ethical obligation: infinite and at every instant" (Derrida 2002, 163). This is why, as Miller informs us, Proust's fascination with Albertine's lie is an incessant reworking of the fissures between the performative and the constative nature of acts of lying and remembrance; the process of realization that says lying is either/ or, distinguishable, separable from some truth or other that can be remembered at a point which says "ah! You were lying when you said that you were in love with her from the beginning," or "I know that you lied when you said you didn't like truffles because you are eating them now."

The problem with the lie, of bearing false witness, is that it necessitates a distinction between speech acts—felicitous and infelicitous, as J. L. Austin would have it—which are not meta-discursively separable, that is, indubitably and epistemologically understandable on a structural level: "Truthful testimony," in Peggy Kamuf's reading of "Plato's Pharmacy,"—and one can only believe that there has ever been any such thing—is conditioned by the possibility that it is false. And this possibility is irreducible. If it were not, then testimony would provide the certainty of a proof, and would, therefore, not be what it is, testimony. To be truly what is called testimony, rather than proof, it must possibly be false, a fiction.[1] If a lie is to be effective as such, at the very moment of its performance, it must be felicitous because it must be taken in its context as truthful; it is taken for the truth because it performs its action and makes something happen. That something can never be known directly and, insomuch as the lie predicates a relation to intention and faith, the lie can only ever be known *to have been* a lie, retrospectively speaking. Like the imperative declensions in my previous quotation from Derrida—that humorously tentative trip from one must to one should—an *obligation* is shown to be a *memory* of fact about which one is never quite sure. Perhaps this may also be said of the act of memory necessitated by my own insinuating imperative that the reader *must . . . should . . .* remember the quotation from Derrida. Here, we have an ethical responsibility to infinite remembrance, an ethical responsibility to an economical accounting for the whole storyline from beginning to end. Like reading Proust's novels or James' somewhat unwieldy periodic sentences, narratives have an odd way of showing this to be the case. They also show us that reading closely is a critical (in the broadest sense of that word) enterprise which affords us a momentary glimpse of the "polylogology" (Miller's word) of all narratives, the many-centeredness of the labyrinth in which we always already come to find ourselves to be. Lying against this is the alogical necessity of lying to ourselves by referring to the anacoluthon as a mere figure of rhetoric.[2]

b

"Having placed in my mouth sufficient bread for three minutes' chewing," begins Flann O'Brien's undergraduate narrator in *At Swim-Two-Birds* with sparkling comic wit, "I withdrew my powers of sensual perception and retired into the privacy of my mind, my eyes and face assuming a vacant and preoccupied expression. I reflected on the subject of my spare-time literary activities. One beginning and one ending for a book was a thing I did not agree with. A good book may have three openings entirely dissimilar and interrelated only in the prescience of the author, or for that matter one hundred times as many endings" (O'Brien 2000, 9). Several ideas are of interest to me in this paragraph because they are intersections that seem fundamental to any practical or theoretical approach to speaking of beginnings.

Every writer knows, as Edward Said has said in his somewhat epic work on the topic, and as my own first teacher of English was wont to drill into the minds of his students, that the beginning is crucial.[3] It inaugurates and opens up an idea, a passageway or vista for what will be to come. In that sense, the beginning in some ways determines the end, "the advanced point is at once beginning and end, it is divided as beginning end; it is the place from which or in view of which everything takes place" (Derrida 1992a, 24). It is, therefore, no coincidence that O'Brien's beginning is really overdetermined by his usage of line imagery to signify the origin in terms of a supplementary or disseminative logic. A pervasive topo-tropological thrust throughout the opening passages of this antinovel (though can any novel be really called an antinovel?) confirms this. The fact is that while O'Brien comments on the importance of thinking about beginnings—really thinking about them, not just chewing on the idea—he begins to express the notion of the beginning as always already a plurality of other moments not present to themselves, of endings, of memories, of trajectories, of interrelationships and intertextualities, of temporal and spatial issues. Indeed, the ending and the beginning appear in the same sentence, and, as he relates, are related or not only by the far-sight of the author who, one expects, knows or intimates where he/she is going from the kernel of thought inhabiting the initiatory moment of inscription. This is what narrative means etymologically, the knowledge (L. "gnarus") of the storyline—a logical impossibility since the complete narrative would have to be suspended in time and known from one end to the other as a vast frozen landscape seen from an elevated prospect.

But this is not entirely the case for Miller's "ana-naratologies."[4] Beginnings are haunted.[5] They are "both inside and outside the narrative at once," requisite upon an antecedent foundation that can only be implied by that momentary breach into being of the narrative line itself, preparatory to anything else. "Narratives are in one way or another expedients for covering over this impossibility, which implies the impossibility of getting started" (RN, 58). They hide their beginnings by becoming part of what follows, or, as in the case above, they indicate that the process of beginning is peculiar and extrinsically challenging to what follows at all points in the narrative line. "In the beginning was the word," says John in the fourth Gospel, and "in the end the world without end" for Stephen Daedalus and the Christian messianic tradition—the great paradoxical anti-*Aufhebung* (Joyce 1992, 626). Beginnings uncannily prefigure an end; the difficulty, as Miller quoting Kierkegaard puts it, is not the problem with the beginning per se, but with the beginning's unstoppable force once it has been initiated. Once the narrative just begins, it seeks a place outside of itself to anchor itself. The beginning, the word, and the logos seek out their *telos* in the infinity of the narrative line and end without end. "The beginning was diacritical" (TNT, 92); "in the beginning there was contretemps."[6]

C

What do we mean when we use the word character? The OED describes it variously as: "A distinctive mark impressed, engraved, or otherwise formed; a brand, stamp"; "a graphic sign or symbol – *esp.* a graphic symbol standing for a sound, syllable, or notion, used in writing or in printing"; "one of the simple elements of a written language; e.g. a letter of the alphabet"; "The series of alphabetic signs, or elementary symbols, peculiar to any language; a set of letters"; "The style of writing peculiar to any individual; handwriting"; "Kind or style of type or printed letter"; "A cabbalistic or magical sign or emblem; the astrological symbol of a planet, etc."; "A symbol, emblem, figure; an expression or direct representation"; "A cipher for secret correspondence." Its figurative senses are listed as: "A distinctive mark, evidence, or token; a feature, trait, characteristic. *arch.* in gen. use"; "One of the distinguishing features of a species or genus"; "The aggregate of the distinctive features of any thing; essential peculiarity; nature, style; sort, kind, description"; "The face or features as betokening moral qualities; personal appearance"; "The estimate formed of a person's qualities; reputation: when used without qualifying epithet implying 'favourable estimate, good repute.'"; "A description, delineation, or detailed report of a person's qualities"; "Recognized official rank; status; position assumed or occupied"; "A person regarded in the abstract as the possessor of specified qualities; a personage, a personality"; "An odd, extraordinary, or eccentric person" [a usage I associate most clearly with North Dublin colloquial speech: 'he's some character that lad']; "A personality invested with distinctive attributes and qualities, by a novelist or dramatist; also, the personality or 'part' assumed by an actor on the stage"; used as a transitive verb, "To engrave, imprint; to inscribe, write." Its etymology is equally diffuse: "ME. *caracterē*, a. F. *caractere*, ad. L. *charactēr*, a. Gr. χαρακτήρ instrument for marking or graving, impress, stamp, distinctive mark, distinctive nature, f. χαράττ_ειν to make sharp, cut furrows in, engrave; or perhaps a refashioning of the earlier F. *caracte* after this. In Eng. it was further assimilated in 16th c. by (fictitious) spelling with *ch*-. (Wyclif used both *caracte* and *caracter*; he may have taken the latter directly from Latin, as Littré cites F. *caractère* only from 15th c. In 16–17th c. often *chàracter*."

What has interested Hillis Miller in these rather wandering definitions is the attention, or lack thereof, to what for all intents and purposes is an improper distinction between the figurative and the literal uses of the word. There is what he calls "an uncomfortable wavering in the apparently clear and unambiguously helpful distinction between figurative and literal" (AT, 56). If we understand the distinction in terms the OED is giving us, that the literal is the thing itself or engraved image in its present materiality, we are sure also to envisage (in a figure of speech) the way that a mark stands for, is a placeholder for, another sign or thing. A character derives its status as character, in a Saussurean sense, because it is part of a system of differences, because it always already names or signifies something else: "The literal is [therefore] irreducibly figurative" (57); it *is* because it figures something *other* than itself. Like Nietzsche's mobile army of metaphors, characters themselves share in the metaphorics of an aboriginal (or ab-aboriginal) ground that can never be known outside of its supplementary context and can only be inferred as reference when the grammar is erroneously taken as natural, not conventional. And like the mechanical alphabetical systematization of this book, which paradoxically highlights connectedness, sequentiality, and dependence in its fragmentations, each character traces the character of its antecedents in an unbreakable family relation. Even if I invent a sign beyond all alphabets, it would still form part of a universal grammar. There is no outside character: "To interpret someone's character (handwriting) is to interpret his character (physiognomy) is to interpret his character (personality) is to interpret his character (some characteristic text he has written), in a perpetual round of figure for figure. To read character is to read character is to read character is to read character" (AT, 58).

In its simplest sense then, what Miller suggests in his reading of the OED's 19 separate entries for "character" is that the categorization of the term into neat distinctions does not hold. But even further still, the attempt by the editors to do so emphasizes the importance of seeing that words always exceed their meaningful relations with other words in a lateral transfer that is never saturable in whatever context. The term "character" is only one instance of this phenomenon, but a particularly helpful one for literary reading because its figurative insistence opens up a number of questions pertaining to issues of anthropomorphic or apostrophic projection (reading the face), repetition (the figure as sign), belief (innate moral worth), inference (allegory), causality (mechanics of grammar), and so on and so forth. The resonance of which leads one back to Paul de Man's perpetually elusive concept that ideology is a confusion between a linguistic and a phenomenal reality with a renewed understanding of the difficulty of what he is actually saying; not, of course, a false consciousness in a vulgar Marxist sense, so much as a necessary confusion. How could it be otherwise?

Siegfried Sassoon says something about this transfer in a poem that works on the possibilities of the terms advanced in the OED entry and can perhaps unravel some of the threads in Miller's yarn:

In me, past, present, future meet
To hold long chiding conference.
My lusts usurp the present tense
And strangle Reason in its seat.
My loves leap through the future's fence
To dance with dream-enfranchised feet.
In me the cave-man clasps the seer,
And garlanded Apollo goes
Chanting to Abraham's deaf ear.
In me the tiger sniffs the rose.
Look in my heart, kind friends, and tremble,
Since there your elements assemble.[7]

Taking character in its most general usage as a character in a novel, poem or play, or as a personality with characteristic traits, Sassoon's poem both accepts and abjures this mode of thinking. There are seemingly two contradictory and equally valid ways of reading what is happening here. One way of reading it is to confirm a kind of centrifugal sovereignty of selfhood; the other is of course centripetal, dynamic, and fluid.

"In me past, present, future meet," like Yeats' "For intellect no longer knows/*Is* from the *Ought*, or *Knower* from the *Known*," puts the self in dialogue with the self: "to hold long chiding conference."[8] In a schizophrenic cleaving of consciousness and desire, the voice tries vainly in one direction to fill up the self with the lusted goal and in the other to follow this desire into an unforeseeable future. The second stanza moves through a more heightened awareness of the impossibility of rationalizing this desire. The "cave-man," presumably ignorant of the condition of the split subject, and an emblem of an insurmountable nostalgia for presence, wrestles with the seer. Which is "Reason" and which desire? Here, we reach the crucible: "And garlanded Apollo goes/Chanting to Abraham's deaf ear." How can this be read? Apollo, Greek god of soberness and judgment and Abraham, father of faith, unwavering follower of God's word (the Word), his *logos*, his Reason, figures an interesting intersection between the cave-man and the seer, jewgreek and greekjew as Joyce put it. Yet again another scenario: in what way is Abraham's ear deaf? Is he deaf to the Apollonian "Reason," of the sobriety and judgmental ability of a unified moral character on the side of faith? Or, alternatively, is he deaf to the command made on his character by his son, by the here and now? Or, furthermore, is Abraham deaf to the Apollonian

because obeying God's command itself is unreasonable, in which
case God is not reasonable, not the Word (*logos*), the Christ of the
New Testament?

Another reversal is yet possible still. In *The Birth of Tragedy*,
Nietzsche inverts my presupposition that the cave-man is the Apolline
and the Seer the Dionysiac:

> Apollo, as an ethical deity [a resonant statement!], demands
> moderation from his followers and, in order to maintain it, self-
> knowledge. And thus the admonitions 'Know thyself' and "Nothing
> in excess!" [Socrates' advice from the Delphic oracle] coexist with
> the aesthetic necessity of beauty, while hubris and excess are
> considered the truly hostile spirits of the non-Apolline realm,
> and hence qualities of the pre-Apolline age, the age of the Titans,
> and the world beyond the Apolline, the world of the barbarians.
> (Nietzsche 1993, 26)

Nietzsche's examination of what he calls the "deification of
individuation" leads to a remarkable insight regarding character.
He says, "For the poet the metaphor is not a rhetorical figure but
a representative image that really hovers before him in place of a
concept. For him, the character is not a whole laboriously assembled
from individual traits, but a person, insistently living before his eyes,
distinguished from the otherwise identical vision of the painter by his
continuous life and action" (1993, 42). Character, in other words, is
volatile, centrifugal, dynamic, living, acting, and becoming, an idea
he will develop in the later work.

"In me the tiger sniffs the rose" refigures the predicament once more
in a final twist. The animal and the spiritual collide. The tiger represents,

as in Blake, an apotheosis of animality, the *principium individuationis*, the sovereign ruler of a sylvan world. The rose by contrast, emblem of Christ's passion, forbearance, faith, and vulnerability, echoes the metaphysical appeal to an ultimate unveiling. The terror expressed in the final lines is dubiously double, winding down to the final oxymoronic embellishment on the theme. "Elements assemble" does not mean either unity or disunity. It means both at once, leaving the poem floundering on a question it is neither willing nor able to provide an answer for. For Miller, analogously, realistic fictions provide a substratum for the working through of these possibilities of character cohesion and dehiscence: "I posit nevertheless the claim that one function of realistic novels is to allow the reader to act out her or his fear that there is no character, while at the same time reaffirming its existence in a new form, beyond its disarticulation" (AT. 143). As Sassoon so concisely puts it: "Look in my heart, kind friends, and tremble,/Since there your elements assemble."

d

What is a just decision?[9] What does it mean to say my/his/her decision was justified? All sorts of intricate and complex ideas are entailed in such enquiries. But, as always with such abstractions, an example is required to afford us an explanation of what this could mean pragmatically. One of the problems, however, with such thinking, is that the example is put in question by the question, that is, the question of "justification" is subtly implied by the decision itself. Take for instance the following extract from Paul Auster's novella "City

of Glass," part of his *New York Trilogy*, which *I have decided* to use
in this instance as an example of decision in literature.[10] Here, our
eponymous detective, Quinn, is attempting to justify a decision to
follow Stillman from the time he arrives at the train station.[11] Bearing
a photograph of his quarry, Quinn scans the emerging crowd and,
in an absurdly mysterious moment, sees two identical figures, each
exactly fitting the photograph he has been given, step off the train.
What happens next, we are told, "defied explanation"; it was beyond
reason. A decision is to be made:

> Quinn froze. There was nothing he could do now that would not
> be a mistake. Whatever choice he made – and he had to make a
> choice – would be arbitrary, a submission to chance. Uncertainty
> would haunt him to the end. . . . Quinn craved an amoeba's body,
> wanting to cut himself in half and run in two directions at once.
> 'Do something,' he said to himself, 'do something now, you idiot.'
> For no reason, he went to his left, in pursuit of the second Stillman.
> (Auster 1992, 58)

A moment later, and for no reason, one expects, since there is none
given, he reverses his decision and follows the other Stillman. This
moment is presented as a kind of Kierkegaardian madness, an
unbearable anxiety in an impossible moment of disseverance between
conscious rationalization and sheer gut-instinct. Quinn's leap of faith
is precisely that, a leap into that uncharted night of nonknowledge.
Though the faith he has had up until that moment in his ratiocinating
powers as a detective is shaken, his retrospective analysis of events
will impose the narrative line of justification for the decision. Like
the train Stillman arrives on, a very fitting metaphor for this episode,

Quinn will inevitably retrace his steps and create reasons for his decision along a causal line arbitrarily reconstructed from these bizarre events. He will, in short, justify his decision retrospectively and create a solid chain of reasons for doing so. But the moment itself, we must not forget, is *crucially* described as a nonsense. This is what detective fictions—what Brian McHale calls "the epistemological genre *par excellence*"[12]—continually do, by playing on the expectations of a readership expecting justified decisions and rational dénouements. From Poe to Paretsky, this has been a staple of the genre. But few have done more to question the logical process, it can perhaps be said (with the remarkable exception of Muriel Spark), than Auster has done.

By referring to himself as an "idiot," Quinn makes his point most succinctly—he is quite simply lost. There is nowhere to turn for help. The ground of decision is baseless, leading to an "experience of the impossible" and a further realization that a true decision is never certifiably just, only retrospectively justifiable after its having already taken place.

This last sentence seems not only peculiar but also wholly counterintuitive. How can we say that a decision is never just? Surely, just decisions are made every day in universities, courtrooms, government institutions, and just about every arena of quotidian social and domestic life. The distinction both Derrida and Miller make between the calculable or programmable and a true decision can help us with this. Like the distinction both make between morality and ethics—where morality is resonant with the law or duty and ethics with justice and singularity—a decision is not what one can easily dissociate from a calculation, and, yet, any decision, if it is truly a decision, questions the very economy of accountability—it is, like

Quinn's predicament, an unaccountable madness for which I must be held accountable.

For both one can never say, "I *am* just" or "he *is* just." One can only say, however ironically, that justice never just *is*. Justice *is* never present in the presentable present. It is always to come, but not in an imminent fashion, some event on the horizon or in the foreseeable future. It is *always* to-come, *à-venir*. This future anterior is tied very closely to the question of decision because a decision never really is an event for Derrida (FD, 20).[13] Its singularity is also a *differantial* matter, unpindownable in a moment of time, therefore not an event in a conventional sense since the moment of decision is a kind of secret. It is also never fully understandable. Why does Quinn make the decision here? We are never told. He just does it and "for no reason." On Miller's reading of Isabel Archer's decisions in *The Portrait of a Lady*, these moments of decision are all "blank place[s] in the narration," where the actual moments are "skipped over." Analogously, Auster's text skips over or avoids the moment and just goes on without explanation. This explanation is left up to the reader as an ethical dilemma. How am I to read the decision? How am I to proffer a justifiable reading? How do I decide when the text doesn't? This requires another leap. You decide, because nobody can do it for you.

***

Every decision is, therefore, divisive and elusive; every decision is a "split decision." Like Caesar's army crossing the Rubicon, it alerts us to a disjointed time, to a rupture in the moment that has always already been. It splits the time into a before and after. That d, lest we forget, is also for deconstruction, which is mad about the decision. There is no certainty in decision-making, just as there is no certainty in reading, in good reading at least. Decisions like true readings are haunted by the other, by the undecidable, by the alogical, by madness, by the perpetual displacement and the scission of the now that never simply is. But that does not mean that we don't have responsibility for our decisions; on the contrary, it means our responsibilities are excessive and untimely, that there is never enough time to make a just decision.

This is why deconstruction is also mad about justice (FD, 23). It is why its a kind of madness that stops short of prescription. It doesn't pretend to know everything; its movements are heterogeneous to formalization and conceptualization. Deconstruction is also humble before the other; it welcomes it, calls it to come; it does everything in its power to open the possibility of the arrival of some other that may or may not come, like a benediction arriving out of nowhere. "I have never had a fundamental project," says Derrida, "and 'deconstructions,' which I prefer to say in the plural, has doubtless never named a project, method, or system" (Derrida 1995, 356). He goes even further elsewhere:

> Deconstruction is not a method for discovering that which resists the system; it consists, rather, in remarking, in the reading and interpretation of texts, that what has made it possible for philosophers to effect a system is nothing other than a certain dysfunction or 'disadjustment,' a certain incapacity to close the system. Wherever I have followed this investigative approach, it has been a question of showing that the system does not work,

and that this dysfunction not only interrupts the system but itself accounts for the desire for system, which draws its *élan* from this very disadjoinment, or disjunction. (Derrida 2002, 4)

It is not a tool kit for approaching all texts in the same way, so I can't go out and learn how to become a deconstructionist. So it worries me that that word "deconstructionist" doesn't appear underlined in red when I type it out on my computer. "Deconstruction is not a school or an ism," says Martin McQuillan, "there is no such thing as deconstructionism: this is a word used by idiots" (Royle 2003a, 24). Perhaps McQuillan is right and it seems a little strong for me to put it that way, but it makes the point doesn't it? There is no ism (singular), no method, pathway, or predetermined goal then, only countermovement, *destinerrance*, *adestination*, *disadjustment*, and *disajointment*. What we call the way is only wandering; method is detour (FD, xv). All those isms are fast becoming wasms, and it's a good thing too, since "deconstruction is nothing more or less than good reading" (ER, 10).

e

In his reading of intersubjectivity in Goethe's *The Elective Affinities*, Miller has the following point to make about interpreting a narrative in which there is an interminable oscillation between a realistic and an allegorical reading:

The lack of a secure ground for reading does not mean that the text is not read. Far from it. But it means that the reading of *Die*

Wahlverwandtschaften is neither exegesis, the extraction of a hidden meaning buried within the text, nor diegesis, the narrative unfolding of a clear meaning from beginning through middle to inevitable end in a 'recognition,' 'anagnorisis.' Any reading is rather an eisegesis, the imposition of a meaning over a substratum that can never be encountered face-to-face, in the presence of the present. The rhetorical name for this act of reading is 'performative catachresis.' What the characters, including the narrator, do in the novel, the reader must perforce again do in reading the novel (AT, 210).

As opposed to exegesis, this archaic word re-figures, if that is the correct way to express what happens in such a realization, the relationship between the *act* of reading and the reading as activated through the force of that double antithetical genitive "of." Any act "of" reading is never a simple one-way activity, as is problematically suggested by the word "exegesis," which in fact in its Greek etymology means to "lead out" [ἐξήγησις], to interpret by exposition and explanation. "Eisegesis," on the other hand, means a reading "into" (Gr. εἰς), the difference being between a radical objectivism and a radical subjectivism. Here is the point where *any* act of reading is seen to tremble at the moment of positing a univocal interpretation.

"Interpretation" is itself one of those strange words that hovers precariously on a similar double antithetical problematic. As Geoffrey Bennington has suggestively pointed out in an essay on the "inter" in words like "inter-action," "inter-course," or "inter-penetration," there is a problematic gap being denied by the prefix.[14] The "inter" joins and it separates at once. It calls attention to itself in the way it puts up a barrier between things, as in words like "inter-pose," "inter-fere," "inter-face." The "inter," therefore, neither fully opens up nor closes down the meaning of a word; instead, it always hovers and becomes itself the boundary or threshold of meaning. Can we then say that we read *into* or *out of* a text? Not substantially. The problem is also suggested in Wilde's Preface to *The Picture Dorian Gray*: "The critic is he who can *translate into* another manner or a new material his impression of beautiful things. The highest, as the lowest, form of criticism is a mode of autobiography" (Wilde 1994, 5) [my emphasis]. An extraordinarily odd phrase this! How can one really "translate into"? In saying that all criticism is disguised autobiography, a radical eisegesis, Wilde is supposing that criticism is a one-way street. You get out of the text what you went there to find. The distinction between this, however, and the eisegesis in the Miller quotation is that there will come a point in interpretation when the reading, if pushed far enough, will run into an aporia, a no-through-road, at which moment a decision will have to be made. The critic's reading at this point is always an eisegesis. Because at that moment the logical becomes alogical. When the exegesis is pushed to its limit, it becomes eisegesis, a catachrestic positing in the void, a monstrous inter-pretation or a leap from an abc to an X.

f

In reading the second preface to Rousseau's *Julie*, Paul de Man comes to a generalization about reading that has fascinated Miller in several important works.[15] Says de Man:

The paradigm for all texts consists of a figure (or system of figures) and its deconstruction. But since this model cannot be closed off by a final reading, it engenders, in its turn, a supplementary figural superposition which narrates the unreadability of the prior narration. As distinguished from primary deconstructive narratives centered on figures and ultimately always on metaphor, we can call such narratives to the second (or the third) degree allegories. Allegorical narratives tell the story of the failure to read whereas tropological narratives, such as the *Second Discourse*, tell the story of the failure to denominate. The difference is only a difference in degree and the allegory does not erase the figure. Allegories are always allegories of metaphor and, as such, they are always allegories of the impossibility of reading – a sentence in which the genitive 'of' has itself to be 'read' as a metaphor. (de Man 1979, 205)

What does it mean to say that "the paradigm for all texts consists of a figure (or system of figures) and its deconstruction" only to conclude that this model can never be "closed off in a final reading"? This is a bizarre statement to say the least. In fact what de Man says in the first sentence is taken away in the second. *All* narratives consist of a figure or a system of figures. We give shape to these narratives in our readings, as the etymology of the word "figure" implies (Latin: *fingere*, to make, confect, shape) (AT, 226). We read narratives by shaping them or "figuring" them out. But, and this is a very large "but" indeed, this figuring out can never be completed. However much the interpreter believes that he or she has gone toward "figuring out the text," that reading only goes to show that the belief in a figurative explication will always be undermined by a further figurative displacement. The latter part of this last sentence is perhaps a good example of the difficulties we are faced with when we come to speak of "figure" in narrative since two contradictory uses are implied. The figure first gives shape but then it takes that shape away. It dis-places. For example, "A word becomes figurative only when it is twisted from its normal use by its placement in a sentence, usually as a substitute for some obvious word" (AT, 228). The placing of one word in place of another is what makes the figure figurative.

Yet, if we follow this logic far enough, we will end up where Nietzsche began his discussion in his seminal essay "On Truth and Lies in an Extra-Moral Sense," namely, in a situation where *all* language is seen as figurative through-and-through. Notice, for instance, that the words de Man uses in the cited (part of a) paragraph are oddly mimicking the sense of figure in the two contradictory senses I've pointed out. The "paradigm" (pattern or shape) and "model" (design, figure) "engender" (make, confect) in their "turn" (re-shape, change or trope), etc. The danger with "reading" figure is that it makes or fabricates the shape of the narrative in a secondary or tertiary manner. The failure to denominate becomes another failure in the secondary or tertiary narratives because those latter narratives are themselves supplementary narrative reconfigurations of that same failure. In other words, "The use of figure to deconstruct figure still remains within the assumption that a text is a system of tropological substitutions. It still assumes that mastery of figures is the key to the interpretation of narrative. It assumes that there is at least one reliable figure, namely the one to deconstruct all the others. Moreover, it turns reading into a reassuringly continuous narrative going from a series of successively demystified mystifications to ultimate disillusioned knowledge, in a familiar totalising sequence" (AT, 241). This means that the "deconstructive" interpretation of the narrative of denomination repeats the initial error of reading as denomination by assuming that the figure or figures it chooses can be seen as a controlling force capable of bringing to light what cannot in fact be brought to light. It imposes order on disorder so to speak; it finds the figure in the carpet, but only by missing the wood for the trees. Such is also the case with the genitive "of," as Miller reads it here, because to say that the "of" is a metaphor announces something about the way metaphor covers up a gap in translation. It, therefore, becomes a catachresis in pointing to a gap in the way knowledge works and language acts.

This example from de Man shows that the reading of figure in narrative is extremely problematic. That reading it shapes the interpretations we make in ways that can show us how a close reading of figure is necessary and at the same time how that reading is a way toward seeing how narratives are inherently *unreadable*, if by that word we suggest the impossibility of a comfortable critical clarity. The more attention given to figures the more difficult will be the job of interpreting.

But something else becomes interesting when we try to "figure out" what's going on in de Man's apodictic reading because, as Miller points out in his own reading of the passage, this passage has followed a reading of Rousseau and is, therefore, in a sense figured by that reading, given its shape by that text. Just as my reading is figured by Miller's. Each reading and rereading is, therefore, refigured by the part of the text it reads just as that reading refigures that primary text in an unending series of substitutions and reconfigurations. The peculiar fact about all of these transpositions is that they change the meaning of de Man's example by shifting it to a new context, as I am changing Miller's reading here. Miller's term for this phenomenon is the "Wellerism theory or travelling theory" (T, 335).

A Wellerism is a variable joke that works on a simultaneous similarity and dissimilarity between contexts; it's an utterance that works as a kind of double entendre. The name stems from Tony and Sam Weller, father and son in Charles Dickens' comic novel *Pickwick Papers*. When Tony is afraid that his son will be married, he says: "it'll be a wery agonizin' trial to me at my time of life, but I'm pretty tough, that's vun consolation as the very old turkey remarked wen the farmer said he wos afeered he should be obliged to kill him for the London market" (T, 129). In popular parlance, the more vulgar Wellerisms are often concluded with the phrase "as the actress said to the bishop."[16] The point, however, is importantly one of control; or, rather, that when one thinks one is using language effectively, concisely and literally, one can never be sure that the context in which the utterance will be delivered will be entirely appropriate—meaning and intention are not synonymous. Reading theory, translating it into a new context, means never being able to foresee what will happen ahead of time.

Theories, however, are of no use unless they are performed as acts of reading on texts, which means they are performative and local events particular to a time and place of interpretation. Translating theory means changing it, refiguring it, or giving it a new face. This model cannot be closed off by a final reading.

g

In what way is the act of writing a violent act? And what would it mean to say that acts of writing or reading are inherently violent? In *Ariadne's Thread* and *Illustration*, Miller follows up this question:

> All the *graph* words – graph itself, paragraph, paraph, epigraph, graffito, and graft, in both botanical and economic senses – go back to words meaning pencil, to inscribe, or the inscription itself: Latin *graphium*, pencil, from Greek *graphion*, pencil, stylus, from *graphein*, to write, derived from the root *gerebh-*, scratch. Grammar, diagram, epigram, and so forth belong to the same family. 'Sign' is from Latin *signum*, distinctive mark or feature, seal. 'Glyph' is from Greek *gluphein*, to carve, from the root gleuph-, to cut, cleave. (AT, 9)

Two kinds of graph are subsequently pursued in *Illustration*: the graphic image and the graph as written word. Each one shares in the etymological heritage outlined above as a blow or a cut which opens up something or exposes it. But both are different in kind. Images represent in the here and now. They show but do not tell in quite the same way as writing tells. Images are suspensions of presence: "A picture, labelled or not, is a permanent parabasis, an eternal moment suspending, for the moment at least, any attempt to tell a story through time" (IL, 66). Novels that contain illustrations are, therefore, as Miller puts it, following Henry James, like gardens "growing two incompatible crops" or they are like plants onto which are "grafted a foreign stock" (IL, 69). Each part is in direct contradistinction to the other. Pictures tell a thousand words precisely because they are not made up of words and passively abide our stories about them. So why the word "graphic" for both verbal and pictorial illustration?

"The light [in any illustration] is produced by the act of cutting" (IL, 94). Cutting, as in the word "engrave," which is a double antithetical word, both opens up and covers over simultaneously. The graphic mark, that is, brings something to light while also covering something up; it uncovers and reveals. Therefore, both forms of illustration, verbal and pictorial, are subject to what Miller calls "a double logos" or dialogism because they are differential within themselves as well as being differential from each other. Each is different from within itself and unique, but not univocal, since they depend on a system of differences to be meaningful. The paradoxical nonrelationality of illustrations, showing and telling, hiding and illuminating, means that each in its own way is untranslatable. But "Grafting is a form of anastomosis" (AT, 166), it opens up something to something else or other, it connects and disconnects, shows difference and dependence, brings to light and obscures in a radical feat of monstrous chiaroscuro. The word "monstrous" here suggests a shining forth, or "unconcealedness" to use a Heideggerian register, what he famously calls in Greek *aletheia* (Truth). The truth of *Illustration*, of its grafting and weaving together image and text, is that both text and image are irreconcilable in a grand theoretical design. Each is singular, unique, and different. Examples are grafts in the sense that they take and violently transfer something from one context to another; they disconnect and reconnect. "Illustrations are falsifying abstractions from the ungraspable idea they never adequately bring into the open. What they bring to light they also hide. Like all illustrations, they leave the idea still out of sight, grimly reposing in the dark" (IL, 150). I offer no example, only an idea.

h

Is there an ethics of hypertext? What would it mean? "A hypertext demands that we choose at every turn to take responsibility for our choices. This is the ethics of hypertext" (BH, 137). So, hypertexts bring the idea of choice to the surface for Miller. They also make it more explicit that the text is a fragile thing that can be changed easily by anyone capable of using a computer to manipulate an online text. I could, for instance, easily copy and paste the letter "i" below and place it where "a" is now, if I should choose to discuss the figure "anastomosis" instead of "anacoluthon." This would take me a matter of seconds. Writing this book may, therefore, be another example of the hypertextual habits of reading Miller discusses in *Black Holes* (BH, 125–39). Instead of following a linear progression from a to b to c, I've been writing this book nonsequentially. I've been picking the letters to write about as they've been making their impressions on me. Likewise, this book, I claim, *should* be read that way. One doesn't need to follow a line here. You can choose your own way around, just as in any act of reading you invariably do.

But is this contrived format really contrived? Not if reading is seen as a performative and not as a constative event. The best place I know of to describe this hypertextual performative phenomenon is the "Choose Your Own Adventure" series of children's stories first published in the late 1970s by Bantham Books. In these works, which

I remember reading with relish as a child, "you" are addressed directly in the second person and asked to make decisions for yourself that will affect the outcome of the story. These decisions are signposted by sentences like: "If you decide to cancel your meeting with Runal and search for Carlos, turn to page 7"; "If you feel that Carlos is OK and go ahead with your plan to meet Runal, turn to page 8" (Montgomery 2006, 5). On each page or so, "you" are asked to make a decision about how the narrative will proceed. "Your" choices, therefore, direct not only the outcome of the story, but also the trajectory that story may take. The remarkable thing about these stories is that when the reader begins to understand that there is more than one storyline to follow, those storylines proliferate beyond the structural signposting conceived of and laid out by the author. Readers then become aware of the decisions they make throughout each reading, that each act of reading is in some sense an event, a new performative happening.

BEWARE AND WARNING!

THESE BOOKS ARE DIFFERENT THAN other books. YOU and YOU ALONE are in charge of what happens in this story. There are dangers, choices, adventures and consequences. YOU must use all of your numerous talents and much of your enormous intelligence. The wrong decision could end in despair & even death. At any time, YOU can go back and make another choice, alter the path of your story, and change its results.

GOOD LUCK![17]

For more on decision, see "d." For more on storylines, see "l."

i

In a stunning display of what seems like the most negligent and purblind selfishness, the hapless Rupert Birkin puts forward his opinions on community and responsibility at a dinner party in the "Breadalby" chapter of Lawrence's *Women in Love*. Birkin is responding to what most of us would regard as a rather benign argument about democratic freedom and core humanitarian values coming from another member of the party. Birkin rigorously counterattacks:

> Every man has hunger and thirst, two eyes, one nose and two legs. We're all the same in point and number. But spiritually there is pure difference and neither equality nor inequality counts. It is upon these two bits of knowledge that you must found a state. Your democracy is an absolute lie – your brotherhood of man is a pure falsity, if you apply it further than the mathematical abstraction. . . . But I, myself, who am myself, what have I to do with equality with any other man and woman? In the spirit, I am as separate as one star is from another, as different in quality and quantity. Establish a state on *that*. One man isn't any better than another, not because they are equal, but because they are intrinsically *other*, that there is no term of comparison. (Lawrence 1996, 125)

We're all the same, more or less, physiologically says Birkin. We are generally born with two eyes, a nose, arms, and legs. We don't, that is, have tails, pouches, or a proboscis. This is what it is to be human, a member of the species. Each one of us is also subject to hunger and thirst and therefore dependent on the world around us for our sustenance and survival. We all go hungry at some stage and we will all eventually die. But that is as far as equality goes. It's as far as Birkin is willing to take his analogies. After that there is only "pure difference." "Each man is an infinitely repellent orb, and holds his individual being on that condition" (Emerson 1960, 61). No Rousseauistic social contracts or brotherhoods of man for Birkin, only *others*.

His notion of community is, therefore, a community of "I"s, unadulterated singularities. Intersubjectivity is a fallacy for him, if by that word we assume a kind of anastomosical communication of subjectivities, a crossing over or leaking into. "In anastomosis the self is always outside itself" (AT, 160); "An anastomosis flows into the vessel it opens, pierces it, and becomes enclosed by it" (AT, 156). This is one reason why we might assume Rupert should have a disastrous relationship with Ursula Brangwen, as does Gerald with Gudrun, since the singular difference between both characters is so strong that it resists any mode of communication, any real crossing over of subjectivities. If each other is every bit other, we might begin to assume that this means that there can be nothing in the way of love, that there can be no common sharing in the relationship between these characters. But, on the other hand, we might also begin to see that because the difference is every bit different, the other is not reduced to the status of the same and is, therefore, never assumed to be understandable and therefore common. A conception of a loving relationship would, therefore, have to be based on an infinite respect for an absolute alterity.

Here is the paradox of what Rupert Birkin has been saying: There is no "brotherhood of man"; therefore, there are only differences which can never be understood in any terms. Moreover, democracy, the ideal of brotherly love as ratified in the emancipatory spirit of fraternity, equality, liberty, is just as misguided in its ethos because it assumes that there can be a consensus where only dissensus reigns. *But*, if I see that every other is every bit other then I, myself, my responsibility, and my relationship with the other, is *absolutely singular*: "One man isn't any better than another, not because they are equal, but because they are intrinsically *other*, that there is no term of comparison." There can be no equality in absolute difference. Equality, brotherhood, fraternity, the implicitly sexist declaration of the revolutionary spirit of democracy, is a disguised form of repression because it reduces the other to the status of the same; it makes it equal. What initially seemed like a selfish attack on the benign has become in a strange reversal the most libertarian and revolutionary defense of an absolute ethics. There is no term of comparison, what exists is unspeakable, unavowable.[18]

j

For Emerson and Nietzsche, as for Miller, the act of reading is a joyful science (*fröhliche wissenschaft*), an activity where the search for ideas in a language charged with meaning is an exercise in *wit*, in all of the various senses of that word.[19] Readers are, therefore, consumed in and surprised by the joy of finding new grounds from which to utter the discovery of what might best be described as the otherness or secrecy of literature. "There is then," as Emerson puts it in his remarkable "American Scholar Address," "creative reading as well as creative writing. When the mind is braced by labour and invention, the page of whatever book we read becomes luminous with manifold allusion. Every sentence is doubly significant, and the sense of our author is as broad as the world" (1960, 69). The idea is also expressed consistently in Miller's President's Columns for the MLA *Newsletter*, "Responsibility and the Joy of Reading," "Responsibility and the Joy (?) of Teaching," and "The Obligation to Write." The joy as he expresses it here "is a sense of insight, freedom and power that comes, when it comes, always as a somewhat surprising and unpredictable effect of reading" (TNT, 297). Three things follow from the notion of joy in reading that Miller is trying to explicate throughout his many books and essays: 1) joy is inextricably tied to a singular event, a surprise or happening for which there can be no prior inside knowledge before it arrives on the doorstep, so to speak—in that sense, reading is extra-institutional, outside the realm of theorization, allergic to it; 2) this joy is also inseparably linked to a responsibility or a demand made on us by this originary event to put that happening into other words, whether we recognize it or not, hence the responsibility of teaching and writing in its most rudimentary sense; 3) and, finally, there is the obligation to take responsibility for what has happened as a result of this doing things with words, even though this doing is something which cannot be fully known or controlled. This joy is excessive. Its power of freedom comes from its power to undo previous "laws" of reading and its effective movement into new unforeseen territories beyond horizons of expectation or preconceptions.

Of course there is a paradox here, a kind of unknowable understanding that this new news will be both surprising and expected. "Reading," as we see in *Versions of Pygmalion*, "should be guided by the expectation of surprise, that is, the presupposition that what you actually find when you read a given work is likely to be fundamentally different from what you expected or what previous readers have led you to expect" (VP, 33). How then can a reading be, in Miller's weirdly oxymoronic insight, some sort of surprising expectation or already expected surprise? How can we say that we are guided in our reading by "the expectation of surprise"?

The answer is given in the MLA *Newsletter*. In writing about reading—a process that occurs for Miller in the margins of the texts we read as we read them, and not necessarily in a material sense since "there is always already writing as an accompaniment of reading"— there is a "first writing." This is an "assertion of mastery over what is strange, idiomatic, unfamiliar, unassimilable in what we are reading," an "apotropaic" process which turns that which is potentially unknowable or alien into what is known by adding it to a customarily stratified system of knowledge. Examples of this are scholarly essays that "translate" literature into commentary and regulate that unfamiliarity by adding it to a tradition of logic and reason acceptable within the modern research university. One other example of this is of course these last few sentences, syntactically building on previous statements in order to condense and assimilate large portions of Miller's work so that the present reader's expectations are building at an even pace toward a final resolution.

This function is crucial to thinking about and explaining what exactly it is that *we* do in a university environment, how *we* in a sense justify our positions. It is how we have been taught to read, and how we continue to be taught to read, weaving and unweaving the figures in the carpet, following Ariadne's thread from the clue to the center of the labyrinth. However, "mixed with the apotropaic act of covering over in the 'first writing,' scribbled so to speak in the invisible ink in the margin of the book we read, there is something else, a submission to what the work itself submitted to. This submission dispossess the reader, appropriates him or her, rather than yielding itself to rationalizing appropriation. This too carries over into the essay, chapter or review, in spite of our best efforts to conceal it. Such carrying over gives, perhaps, the chief interest and value to what we write" (TNT, 302). No doubt a counterintuitive claim this!

The secondary process, which Miller is here calling primary, is seen as being relegated to a secondary position by an institution whose primary goal is (or should be) to announce the news of this incoming otherness. Strange to think that it is the illogicality of the act of reading/writing that is uppermost in this joyful activity and (perhaps) lowermost in what we customarily think of as the *raison d'être* of university teaching and learning. And yet, this "secondary writing," lying as it does outside of the laws of conventional wisdom on the subject of criticism, and issuing if you will from the schism between what constitutes literary and literary critical writing, relays the problematic assumption that there is somewhere between the primary and secondary writing which is outside of the linguistic imagination, a thing in itself to be understood, a final surprise or expectation, what Miller following James calls a "field of untrodden snow." There is, therefore, a "perpetual inadequacy" in the act of reading, a knowledge that the "thing" that called the first piece of writing into being, a result of a first response to something ungraspable, something other or strange, and for which that first writing is an inadequate adjunct, necessarily curbs the ability of the commentary to rest assured in its response.

But this is also part of the joy of reading. It is the inadequacy that spurs the reader to keep on reading in a perpetually deferred moment of final clarity; the aporetic fugacity of the act of reading we might say impassions as it flees. The critical re-action generates from this schism the freedom it desires: "If the art of criticism is an art of growth and flowering which becomes an art of flying, a way of doing levitation with words, as a blossom becomes butterfly, this lighter-than-air feat uses the text it criticises as but a mountaintop airfield from which to take off" (ER, 119). The discrepancy between the two kinds of secondary writing, the rendering power of rational response and the noncognizable response to the strangeness of the work itself, keeps these lines of appropriate response interminably blurred. Thus, the two kinds of reading/writing also blur into each other interminably; teleological desire becomes subservient, giving way to a reading drive, a delight in the journey, not the final destination, an infinite peripatetic wandering or Kantian purposiveness without purpose, as Juliet Flower MacCannell puts it in *Provocations to Reading*, "J is for *Jouissance*" (13). J is for the joyful science of the active soul, the Emersonian-Nietzschean-Millerian flux.

k

'I Michael Henchard, on this morning of the sixteenth of September, do take an oath here in this solemn place that I will avoid all strong liquors for the space of twenty years to come, being a year for every year that I have lived. And this I swear upon the Book before me; and may I be stricken dumb, blind and helpless if I break this my oath.'

When he had said it and kissed the big book, the hay-trusser
arose, and seemed relieved at having made a new start in a new
direction. (Hardy 1997, 18)

Henchard has of course, in a drunken stupor, just sold his wife and
child at the Weydon-Priors Fair to a sailor by the name of Newson.
He will later confide to the young Scotsman Donald Farfrae that
because of drinking, he "did a deed on account of it which I shall
be ashamed of till my dying day (sic). . . . I have kept my oath; and
though, Farfrae, I am sometimes that dry in the dog days that I
could drink a quarter-barrel to the pitching, I think o' my oath,
and touch no strong drink at all" (48). That oath has been sealed,
as we say, with a kiss. The promise Henchard makes to himself and
to God only comes about, Hardy informs us, when the Bible he is
holding is kissed. There's no going back from that moment. When
his lips touch the cover of the "big book," the performative act has
taken place, the oath has been made.

Miller has quite a bit to say about kisses in his work.[20] Notably in an
essay on Kafka's *Letters to Milena*, "Thomas Hardy, Jacques Derrida,
and the 'Dislocation of Souls,'" in which he draws our attention to the
way Kafka has said that "written kisses don't reach their destination,
rather they are drunk on the way by the ghosts" (TPP, 171). These
ghosts drink the kisses in letters because the soul that writes letters is
dislocated in an uncanny way. Writing makes one into a being two-
to-speak, doubling the "I" that writes and the "I" that is written. I
write "I." I am dislocated. Somewhere in-between awaits a host of
phantoms waiting to make my message to my loved one a message
to you: XXX.

A BEFORE B—OF COURSE...   37

What is a kiss? Miller asks time and again. There is no easy answer to this question. "With the exception of Novalis," says Derrida, "there has rarely been, to my knowledge, an attempt at *thinking*, what is called thinking, the kiss" (Derrida 2005a, 306). One even wonders if Derrida is blowing a kiss to Heidegger in saying this? At any rate, thinking about the kiss becomes difficult when speculation about it takes place under the assumption that each kiss is in some way a unique act. What for instance does it mean to say that someone is a "bad kisser"? An appellation that I remember being among the most destructive slurs a secondary schoolboy could possibly incur from one of the local girls. Can anyone really be said to be bad at something which is most often, if not always, significantly different each time it takes place? Kissing one's mother or sister, or the French *bise* between members of the same sex, is surely different, for instance, from kissing one's sexual partner.

A kiss can mean so many different things that I confine myself to my example. What happens when Henchard kisses the Bible? The problem with that kiss is that it is both a constative and performative sign act. "A kiss is a way of doing things not with words but with signs," says Miller, but "there is nothing particularly against standard speech act theory in saying this. Austin in *How to Do Things with Words* allows for the possibility of such wordless words, as when a judge condemns a man with a gesture rather than with speech" (LC, 32).

Henchard's wordless word will be kept for the space of 20 years. He will remain true to his oath. That kiss will, therefore, have been effective in making something happen in history. The kiss, we might say, is the outward expression of an inner decision. "I Michael Henchard," etc., doesn't really mean anything until the sign act accompanies

the speech act. And yet we can say that both sign act and speech
act are doing the same thing. They are both promises. Everything in
the novel arguably follows from Henchard's moment of kissing the
Bible. The subtitle of the novel is an indication of how this kiss makes
and breaks Henchard: "The Life and Death of a Man of Character."
That kiss is both life-giving and life-denying in a myriad of different
ways. The moment that Henchard becomes a man of character is the
moment he confirms his allegiance to an oath made to himself and to
God. The moment that oath is fulfilled is the moment that Henchard
will hasten on toward death. In short, that kiss is perhaps the most
important moment in the novel. And it is a moment that any reading
of the novel cannot fail to take into account. Reading the kiss in *The
Mayor of Casterbridge* is the impossible possibility about which the
entire narrative winds, evolves, and revolves. What is a kiss?

1

L is for line, in case you can't follow. In a particularly philosophic
moment, Melville's Ishmael pauses to reflect in finely wrought
sentences on the disparity between the smooth ocean surface under
the Pequod's small whaling boats and the "remorseless fang" concealed
beneath the "velvet paw" of the sea. Below an ablated sun and adrift in
the dreamy quietude of a windless day, he speaks of its effects on the
spirits of the crew:

> Oh, grassy glades! oh, ever vernal endless landscapes in the soul;
> in ye, – though long parched by the dead drought of the earthy

life, – in ye, men yet may roll, like young horses in new morning clover; and for some few fleeting moments, feel the cool dew of the life immortal on them. Would to God these blessed calms would last. But the mingled, mingling threads of life are woven by warp and woof: calms crossed by storms, a storm for every calm. There is no steady unretracing progress in this life; we do not advance through fixed gradations, and at the last one pause:– through infancy's unconscious spell, boyhood's thoughtless faith, adolescence' doubt (the common doom), then skepticism, then disbelief, resting at last in manhood's pondering repose of If. But once gone through, we trace the round again; and are infants, boys, and men, and Ifs eternally. Where lies the final harbor, whence we unmoor no more? In what rapt ether sails the world, of which the weariest will never weary? Where is the foundling's father hidden? Our souls are like those orphans whose unwedded mothers die in bearing them: the secret of our paternity lies in their grave, and we must there to learn it. (Melville 1993, 411)

The title of this short impressionistic chapter of Melville's master-piece is "The Gilder." Used as an adjectival noun, the word means "someone who gilds," that is someone who covers, plates, or otherwise adorns something in gold or some other precious metal. It can also mean to give inordinate praise to someone or something. "Gilding" means softening down or making something unpleasant pleasant. In this sense, Hamlet accuses Ophelia in a vicious sentiment of gilding: "I have heard of your paintings too, well enough," says he, "God hath given you one face, and you make yourself another" (3:1:146–7). It has, therefore, connotations of a wilful or deceitful subterfuge, a covering up of something ugly or unseemly, and also a covering over of one's true intentions below a veneer of ingenuousness. It means in popular parlance being "two-faced," a whited sepulchre. The metaphor is consequently extended to the fact that the calm seas are likewise a gilded beauty: "The long-drawn virgin vales; the mild blue hill-sides; as over these their steals the hush, the hum; you almost swear that play-wearied children lie sleeping in these solitudes, in some glad Maytime, when the flowers of the woods are plucked" (411). We are aware, of course, like our narrator and Ahab, that the beauty is layer-thin, that the depths are replete with demonic leviathans, but we choose for a brief moment to forget this and are entranced by the luminous gleam of the serene waters. The biblical reference is also unmistakable: "And the earth was without form, and void; and darkness *was* upon the face of the deep. And the spirit of God moved upon the face of the waters" (Genesis 1:2). At the close of the chapter, Starbuck murmurs "Let faith oust fact; let fancy oust memory; I look deep down and do believe" (412).

But the primary passage speaks of a loss of faith in the possibility of escaping the basic fact that the "threads of life are woven by warp and woof," that the calmnesses are following on the heels of storms, that façade conceals chaos. Used as a proper noun, a "gilder" is a snare, especially for catching birds (OED). This is suggestive of the way the sea as it is figured in the entire chapter is like a soporific balm luring weary mariners not to wander more. The narrator's sobriety is a striking antidote to the arguments Tennyson's sailor's put forth in the "The Lotos-Eaters": "Death is the end of life; ah, why/Should life all labour be?" (Tennyson 1959, 21). Our narrator's firm answer is that the condition of all things is delicately poised between torture and toil.

But what is most interesting here is what the narrator makes of the line from birth to death: "There is no steady unretracing progress in this life; we do not advance in fixed gradations, and at the last one pause." What follows from this is a series of possibilities from blithe infancy, adolescent doubt and skepticism, to disbelief and agnostic "Ifs." Once we reach this "If" stage, we are being led to believe, we have no peace, since the "If" is no repose. "If" is a faithless faith, or a positionless position, so to speak. Doubt is the father of a foundling philosophy in which the narrator can, if ever, only conclude that the vibrating line between faith and knowledge can only settle in death. However, there is no way of knowing whether this will be the case because as in life there is, as in death, no pause upon which to perch a solution. Death may be the end of the line, but it is no assurance that the line has successfully run its course, that it has found its logos. Death, therefore, is another "If," perhaps the grandest of them all, and the point to which Ishmael's and Melville's stories are directed. "The secret of our paternity," we are told, "lies in their grave, and we must there to learn it." Notice that the secret lies somewhere else. Not in *our* death but in *theirs*, though we must there to learn it. Where? There. This is a complicated doubling. Another use of the word "gilder" the OED tells me comes from angling, a usage one would assume all mariners would be familiar with. Here, the term describes the process of making a fishing line by entwining different lines, such as strands of horsehair, and binding them together. It also refers to the links in the line where these strands are joined to lengthen the fishing line. "The Gilder" is, I claim, a chapter about storytelling, its warp and woof. It is a story within a story about the way all stories are stories about faith and knowledge, and how any story about these possibilities ("Ifs") finds its true ground in death. *If* Miller is right, this means that "death is the hidden ground of all speech acts" and Melville is once more lying against death (LC, 223).

m

Here's another example Melville gives us of the figure of the line in narrative. This time from *Billy Budd*:

> In this matter of writing, resolve as one may to keep to the main road, some bypaths have an enticement not readily to be withstood. I am going to err into such a bypath. If the reader will keep me company I shall be glad. At the least, we can promise ourselves that pleasure which is wickedly said to be in sinning, for a literary sin the divergence will be. (Melville 2001, 460)

Later the narrator of this tragic story of the "Handsome Sailor," will tell us "His portrait I essay, but shall never hit it" (466); and later still of the snide master-at-arms: "for the adequate comprehending of Claggart by a normal nature these hints are insufficient. To pass from a normal nature to him one must cross 'the deadly space between.' And this is best done by indirection" (474). That "deadly space between" has already been figured by Melville's bypaths. The assumption that there is a main road from which to digress underlies the narrative structure, its logocentricity. "The proper structure of the Plot" of a tragedy, Aristotle holds in the *Poetics*, must be "complete" and "whole." "A whole is that which has a beginning, a middle, and an end." Beginnings we are told do not "follow anything by causal necessity." An ending, contrariwise, "is that which itself naturally follows some other thing, either by necessity, or as a rule, but has nothing to follow it." A middle, however, "is that which follows something as some other thing follows it" (Aristotle 1932, 31). In "White Mythology," Derrida picks up Aristotle's use of the word "proper" in the *Poetics*. "The necessity of examining the history and system of the value of "properness" has become apparent to us," he says. "An immense task, which supposes the elaboration of an entire strategy of deconstruction and an entire protocol of reading. One can foresee that such a labor, however far off it may be, in one fashion or another will have to deal with what is translated by 'proper' in the Aristotelian text" (Derrida 1986a, 246).

Billy Budd, likewise, questions this "proper" or "normal" relation in narrative in its own unique way, asking of its readers to address the questions: what is the proper pathway? Can it be seen or defined in Aristotelian terms? And, can there be such a thing as a literary sinning? The *Poetics* is the precursor text of structuralist works on the subject of the proper reading. Both attempt to provide answers, white mythologies if you like, for what those protocols must be. "Here is the reason," they say, "the ground from which the 'proper' reading originates." But, if we look more closely at Melville's example, it works on a deferred action, a promise of something to come and a memory of something that has always already passed us by. "I *am* going to err"; "we can promise ourselves." These come four chapters into the narrative. Melville has already erred in his direction. The literary sinning of which he enthuses has already been happening. He's in the middle of his delight in disorder. Literature, he is telling us, is im-proper, "A careless shooe-string, in whose tye I see a wilde civility" (Herrick 1920, 26).

n

"Let us note in passing," says Derrida at one point in *Writing and Difference*, "that the concepts of *Nachträglichkeit* and *Verspätung*, concepts which govern the whole of Freud's thought and determine all his other concepts, are already present and named in the *Project* [*Project for a Scientific Psychology* (1895)]. The irreducibility of the 'effect of deferral' – such, no doubt, is Freud's discovery" (Derrida 1978, 203). *Nachträglickeit* names a deferred effect, a deferred event, or after-effect. It names what happens after an event has happened already in the past and happens again in the present. It names, in short, something that has always already happened or has happened always already, a deferred event as the displaced return of the repressed. Its timing is odd or strange, a kind of *déjà vu*. Indeed, Freud might be said to be the master of the *déjà vu*, the uncanny time of the after-effect.[21]

Falling in love belongs to this strange time of *Nachträglichkeit*. "The beginning, the moment of falling in love, is not presented by Trollope when it occurs," says Millers, "just as, according to Marcel [in Proust's *opus*], we do not experience the first moment of a love as the beginning of a new love: 'When one wants to remember in what manner one began to love a woman, one is already in love with her.' That first moment does not, apparently, exist as something that could be presented, since it was not present when it was present. It only exists after the fact, like a childhood or adult trauma that only becomes traumatic later on, after the fact, through what Freud calls 'Nachträglichkeit'" (RN, 156).

How then can I ever know that I *am* in love, if love begins after the fact? How can I say that I was in love from the beginning, if that beginning is never present? The moment of falling in love for Miller is like a black hole, a postulated idea of something that exists as a deferred effect itself. The beginning of love is a secret. It is a secret in the strong sense of the word: something that can never be known. "Falling in love, it could be argued, is, quite strictly speaking, a form of trauma and of performative events generally. Such events do not occur when they occur. They occur only later on, in retrospect, at the moment when they are granted originating power by a speech act like Ayala's 'I always loved you,' or her 'Lady Albury, I think I fell in love with him the first moment I saw him,' or her 'I declare that I always loved him'" (BH, 299).

This is very peculiar indeed, since the suggestion that the performative aspect of speech acts have "originating" power indicates that I can only be in love after I have said "I am in love" or "I love you." Is "I love you" a constative or a performative statement? There is no way of knowing this for sure, because every "I love you" is groundless, queered, if you will, between the expression and the always absent beginning. "I love you" brings into being what it names because it is a form of doing things with words, an act. But at the same time saying "I love you" ought to be measured on a constative basis, we should know that it is either a true or a false statement. Either "I love you" or I don't. Miller's point in discussing this speech act in Trollope and Derrida is that the expression is a good example of the aporia between use and mention. When I say "I love you" here, I am placing it in inverted commas in order to signify that I am mentioning the phrase. When Miller does so, he is ostensibly doing the same thing. But the possibility is always present in any "I love you" that I may not be merely mentioning. Every "I love you" gets its power from the fact that it is the repetition of a common phrase and at the same time a singular speech event: I love you. It also gains its power by the troubling possibility that its mention may never be simply that.

In *Wuthering Heights*, the strange *Nachträglichkeit* of falling in love becomes an explicit theme when Catherine returns from Thrushcross Grange to tell Nelly in secret that she has accepted Edgar Linton's proposal of marriage. Heathcliff is of course listening to the conversation in the background. Nelly asks Catherine if she loves Edgar. Catherine says "Of course I do." "Then," says Nelly to Mr Lockwood, "I put her through the following catechism: for a girl of twenty-two, it was not injudicious.

> 'Why do you love him, Miss Cathy?'
>
> 'Nonsense, I do – that's sufficient.'
>
> 'By no means; you must say why?'
>
> 'Well, because he is handsome, and pleasant to be with.'
>
> 'Bad!' was my commentary.
>
> 'And because he is young and cheerful.'
>
> 'Bad, still.'
>
> 'And because he loves me.'
>
> 'Indifferent, coming there.'
>
> 'And he will be rich, and I shall like to be the greatest woman of the
>   neighbourhood, and shall be proud of having such a husband.'
>
> 'Worst of all. And now say how you love him?'
>
> 'As everybody loves – You're silly, Nelly'"
>
> (Brontë 1992, 55–6).

Catherine's subsequent realization that she "loves" Edgar Linton for selfish reasons and that it would "degrade" her if she married Heathcliff are consequences of Nelly's so-called catechism. Ultimately, however, and as we see later in the novel, Nelly's attempt to make Catherine see reason will be ineffective. Catherine will marry Edgar while Heathcliff is away making his fortune in order to win her respect. But does he need to win her love? No. Catherine professes that she loves Heathcliff before Nelly admits to having noticed him furtively escaping out the back. The salient reason for Heathcliff's departure is, as Nelly makes clear, that Cathy has said that it would degrade her to marry him.

The time of Catherine's loving is then given in the somewhat enigmatic lines:

> My love for Linton is like the foliage in the woods: time will change it, I'm well aware, as winter changes the trees. My love for Heathcliff resembles the eternal rocks beneath: a source of little visible delight, but necessary. Nelly, I *am* Heathcliff! He's always, always in my mind: not as a pleasure, any more than I am always a pleasure to myself, but as my own being (59).

Something beyond the pleasure principle we might imagine. But why the repetition of always? "He's always, always in my mind"? If we heard someone say this, depending on the intonation and context, we might infer that they were lying, inventing, or otherwise hesitating to say what they mean. We might say that they were smoothing over a gap of some sort. Surely, one "always" will suffice. Nevertheless, the strange movement of Catherine's annunciation of eternal love for Heathcliff is odd because of the tenses employed to make her point, the *way in which* she makes it. "I *am* Heathcliff," I have always, always loved him. Catherine's proclamation of love for Heathcliff, I claim, is, therefore, an expression of love as a traumatic event in a time-out-of-time. It is *Nachträglichkeit*. All the references to the question of love in the novel are a kind of catechism, a question-and-answer process in an endless spiraling, nonsublative dialectic. Catherine can never say why she loves either Heathcliff. That's the point. The event of Catherine's realization of her love for Heathcliff, her self-realization is news of the always already, a time out of joint with itself. Catherine *is* haunted by Heathcliff—always has been and always will be.

O

All of Miller's readings, if viewed from a certain point on the horizon, are like prayers. They are openings to something to come, waiting with a nonpassive endurance for something to happen. "A poem," he says, "comes by fate or by chance. It 'befalls' the one who receives it, like words that confer a blessing or that invoke a blessing. Benediction means, literally, speaking well, usually of some person or thing. A benediction invokes what comes from the other or is the coming of the other, subjective and objective genitive at once" (O, 170). What happens, what comes, what is given from or to the other is a blessing. It is an invocation, an act of calling to the other, and a prayer to the other, a way of saying yes to the other. "To pray is to open one's mouth and say 'yes.' To pray is to open one's mouth and say 'come.' Let something Other, something In-coming, come: *l'invention de l'autre*" (Caputo 1997, 298).

Miller is constantly praying for the invention of the other, doing everything he can to prepare for its coming, inventing languages for it, bending language to it, trying not to render the other the same. Because "to read creatively in an attempt to respond fully and responsibly to the alterity and singularity of the text is to work against the mind's tendency to assimilate the other to the same, attending to that which can barely be heard, registering what is unique about the shaping of language, thought, and feeling in this particular work. It involves a suspension of habits, a willingness to rethink old positions in order to apprehend the work's inaugural power . . . there is no single 'correct' reading, just as there is no single 'correct' way for an artist, in creating a new work, to respond to the world in which he or she lives" (Attridge 2004, 80).

Miller will always have said "yes" to a call, *his* call from the other to come. It will, therefore, be a unique response, something singular, an act that will act on its own, by its own, on behalf of its own unheard-of demand. This demand comes from the books that have fallen into Miller's hands fortuitously over the years, by chance and fate. He will have said "yes" to their callings when he has responded to their illimitable alterity, when he has pushed the encounter to the limits of rationalization and found what is peculiar, odd, about their demands on him. The others' demands, that is. Miller surprises his readers because he himself is surprised by joy, by a joy as impatient as the wind. Bless my soul! is that what that is? Saying "yes" to the other, that is what Miller is best at. That is his benediction. *Benedictus qui venit in nomine Domini* [Blessed be he that cometh in the name of the Lord]. Blessed is he who can speak well of the other, who says "yes" to the other:

Everyone suddenly burst out singing;
And I was fill'd with such delight
As prison'd birds must find in freedom

Winging wildly across the white

Orchards and dark-green fields; on; on; and out of sight.

Everyone's voice was suddenly lifted,

And beauty came like the setting sun.

My heart was shaken with tears; and horror

Drifted away . . . O but everyone

Was a bird; and the song was wordless; and the singing will never

   be done.

(Sassoon 1943a, 1133–4)

p

"A title is always a promise," says Derrida (1986a, 115). It always says more or less than what it means to say. When I promise to provide you with the "abc of good reading," I am making a promise that I cannot possibly keep. I may not have been serious when I said it, or, alternatively, I may have intended to do just that, provide you with the alpha and omega of narrative terminology. But either way this will not happen. I have made a lying promise. Sorry. But a promise is a promise and I must be held accountable as J. L. Austin would have us believe. I must be held responsible: *my word is my bond*. Shylock-like, Austin is for the law of the bond. Once I say "I promise," I "do" it. I promise. I give my word, as Derrida does when he speaks of the meaning of a "given word" in *Memoires for Paul de Man*. Elsewhere, in "The Villanova Roundtable" to be precise, he puts it like this:

> As soon as you address the other, as soon as you are open to the
> future, as soon as you have a temporal experience of waiting for

the future, of waiting for someone to come: that is the opening of experience. Someone is to come, is *now* to come. Justice and peace will have to do with this coming of the other, with the promise. Each time I open my mouth, I am promising something. When I speak to you, I am telling you that I promise to tell you something, to tell the truth. Even if I lie, the condition of my lie is that I promise to tell you the truth. So the promise is not just one speech act among others; every speech act is fundamentally a promise. (Caputo 1996, 23)

So, every time I open my mouth I say "yes" to the promise, even when I lie or am being most negative. "*Die Sprache verspricht (sich)*" is Paul de Man's most explicit formulation of the promise (1979, 277). It means language promises and also that language makes a slip of the tongue. Language, he says, conveys the promise of its own truth. It promises. But it only promises itself. "*Die Sprache verspricht (sich)*; language promises and at the same time contradicts itself, misspeaks, makes a slip of the tongue. Austin wanted at all costs to avoid reaching de Man's somewhat scandalous conclusion, though it was the center of the swamp on whose periphery he remained bogged down" (SA, 174).[22] Language fundamentally misspeaks the promise of the future. Its double call is for an impossible future, a future anterior, an other future, a messianic future without messiah that will always be coming, a future that can never arrive, a future we will always already be waiting for.

For Derrida is the title Miller has given to his long book on Derrida. But what does he promise? What is Miller waiting for in this titular promise? What (im)possible futures guide his hand in writing *for*

Derrida? *To* whom and *for* whom does he write? The title becomes a riddle bursting open like a desiccated seed pod when we try to read it conscientiously. It is a play on a slippage in semantics and translation that cannot be stilled. That "for" acts as a preposition reaching out toward something one cannot really ever fully grasp. That "for" is extensive, prosthetic, longing.

On one level, Miller's book is *for* Derrida, he informs us, in being dedicated to his memory. The essays within the book—each one of which a singular response, a micrological act of reading—are also advocating his memory; they are *for* Derrida in being behind him, recommending him and defending him. Miller's book is also a faithful memoir of 40 years of unclouded friendship, an "impossible," "endless," "absolute" act of mourning that hasn't worked (FD, 326). In remembering Derrida, Miller is speaking for him, on his behalf, for 40 years and more. In this latter sense, the book is an act of ventriloquism because Miller must, in Derrida's absence, give voice to his works and by voicing them make them live on.

In French, the words "*for*," "*fors*," and "*fort*" are homonyms. In the translator's introduction to Derrida's *The Post Card*, Alan Bass teases out some of the implications of these words for Derrida's readers:

> *Le for* derives from the Latin *forum*, tribunal, and is most often used in the sense of *le for intérieur* (literally 'the interior forum'), meaning conscience, the depths of oneself. That *le for* has come to have the sense of inner depths is etymologically paradoxical, since forum itself comes from *foris*, meaning outside. A *forum*, of course, was an outdoor place for legal and commercial business. The somewhat archaic French preposition *fors*, from *foris*, means

'except,' 'save,': whatever is left out. (*Fors* is the title of Derrida's preface to Torok and Abraham's *Le verbier de l'homme aux loups*; it describes the paradoxical nature of the crypt as something secret and open, inner and outer, perhaps like a crypted letter whose message is as private and public as that on a post card.) *Un fort* is either a fort (where guards are posted) or a strong person. *Fort* as an adjective or adverb means strong, but in more ways than in English. For example, to be good at a particular subject is to be *fort*; to take one's assurance or confidence from a given precondition is *être fort de*. The French *fort* in all these senses is to be taken in conjunction with the German *fort*, meaning 'away' or 'gone,' as in *fort da*. (Derrida 1987, xxii)

How then to read the promise of this title? How to read this given word—the gift of this word? There are so many possibilities and all promised at the same time. *For Derrida* also opens up another peculiar question of translation, since on an auditory level we cannot even be sure if we are to read this title in French or in English: Derrida's strength, Derrida's remains, Derrida in public and in private, the secrecy of Derrida, Derrida's crypt, Derrida gone, and (by association, in the movement between the German *fort* and *da*) Derrida here, reading Derrida now. All of these are cooperating in that simple, concise formulation that seems in opening up to promise itself to an infinite reading. One can also imagine an exclamation in the title, as golfers might use when they cry out "fore!" on the golf course in order to prepare you for something unexpected and perhaps not all that welcome. Miller speaks of this in his interview with Dragan Kujundžić in the film

The First Sail. There he speaks of trying to bring out a darker side of Derrida's later thinking in *For Derrida* which he associates with self-destructive suicidal tendencies at work in Derrida's politics of autoimmunity.

Though that "for" is certainly "forward" moving, propelling us toward an affirmation at work everywhere in Derrida and also of course in Miller. It is a great Nietzschean and Joycean "yes!" It is surely not fortuitous that Miller chooses to end his latest book, a book weighted heavily on that extensive preposition, *Reading for our Time*, with that word "yes." "'For' signals therefore," says Julian Wolfreys, "with a singularity that is very much the signature of J. Hillis Miller, a seeking-after of a reading to come in another time, in other times, other tempi, in the other's time" (RT 2012, ix).

As the title promises, it also makes a slip of the tongue by giving itself up to the future. A title can never close down the work of reading. On the contrary, titles give themselves up to readers to come, to better readings. The promise says yes to the future, and yes again to the past, in a double act of affirmation, not one "yes" but "yes, yes." "Deconstruction," says Derrida, "is 'yes' . . . When I say 'yes,' I immediately say 'yes, yes.' I commit myself to confirm my commitment in the next second, and then tomorrow, and then the day after tomorrow" (Caputo 1996, 27). I am responsible to the memory of my yes, to the memory of my primary affirmation, to the promise of a tomorrow. Reading is like this because it promises and promises again, always in the singularity of the moment of reading, always inaugurating the new, anew. The title promises the new each and every time I read it; it promises a reading to come, for tomorrow, and tomorrow, and tomorrow. Yes.

q

In his chapter on Gerald Manley Hopkins in *The Disappearance of God*, Miller speaks of Hopkins' expression for self-awareness: "The proof of selfhood is a matter of tasting not thinking," he says (DG, 271).[23] Hopkins' version of the Cartesian *Cogito* is, therefore, a radical formation of alterity: "I taste myself, therefore I am, and when I taste myself I find myself utterly different from everything else whatsoever" (DG, 271). This opens up an impossible predicament. How can one know another if one can never know oneself? "My selftaste is, literally, 'unspeakable'. Words, those counters of shared experience, will not describe it. Only if another man could be in my skin could he know how it tastes to be me" (271). Bottom says something similar in *A Midsummer Night's Dream*:

> I have had a most rare vision. I have had a dream past the wit of man to say what a dream it was. Man is but an ass if he go about t'expound this dream. Methought I was – there is no man can tell what. Methought I was, and methought I had – but man is but a patched fool if he will offer to say what me thought I had. The eye of man hath not heard, the ear of man hath not seen, man's hand is not able to taste, his tongue to conceive, nor his heart to report what my dream was. I will get Peter Quince to write a ballad of this dream. It shall be called 'Bottom's Dream', because it hath no bottom, and I will sing it in the latter end of a play, before the Duke. (4.1, 202–15)[24]

Bottom's dream is bottomless because it is unspeakable. The series of synesthetic references are part of the problem of what it would mean to put Bottom's selftaste into words. What would it mean to say that a man's hand hath not tasted? Or a man's tongue hath not conceived? Something in the way of a problematics of touch, of autoaffection, or selftouch, is at work here to undo an interpretation, a finality of rationalizing, an answer to what the dream of the self means. The senses are garbled in such a way that the very idea of putting into words what can only be sensed indirectly becomes deferred. Bottom will have someone else, Peter Quince, write a ballad, a poetic narrative, about why no one's hand can taste the dream of his selftaste.

"How to accede to the 'taste of myself' of another?" asks Derrida in an essay on Miller's reading of selftaste in Hopkins. "How to feel or get a sense of the 'taste of myself' of a very close friend, when proximity does not prevent the altogether close from remaining also an unknown? This is the question that has constantly plagued me during this long life of friendship I have had the unique chance to share with J. Hillis Miller" (Cohen and Kujundžić 2005, 230). Questions like "Who is J. Hillis Miller?" "What does he think?" "What does he do?" follow from the question what is the selftaste of J. Hillis Miller? "What is the singular and solitary taste one feels in contact with oneself, at every moment when one is oneself J. Hillis Miller?" (2005, 239). The univocity of being, the selftaste of the being-alone-with-oneself, its taste, is a queer ontology. "To be is to be queer," says Derrida (2005a, 243). And, dare I say it, Miller *is* queer. His singularity as a just reader of literary works, always on the lookout for just what happens [*ce qui arrive*], makes him queer. He is alone in his queerness, belonging without belonging to an untouchably queer poetics, an ananarratology. There is no "we" in "queer." No qwer. My own selftaste is a queer thing in a disjointed queer and now.

Derrida's extraordinarily beautiful lines from his late seminars on Robinson Crusoe make this point most succinctly:

> Between my world, the 'my world,' what I call 'my world,' and there is no other for me, every other world making up part of it, between my world and every other world, there is initially the space and the time of an infinite difference, of an interruption incommensurable with all the attempts at passage, of bridge, of isthmus, communication, translation, trope, and transfer that the desire for a world and the sickness of the world [*mal du monde*], the being sickness of the world [*l'être en mal du monde*] will attempt to pose, to impose, to propose, to stabilize. There is no world, there are only islands (FD, 121, 181; CC, 26).

That I am different from others in my world, what I call my world, says Derrida, repeating again that enthralling phrase over and over, allows us to catch a glimpse of Derrida's belief that I am also other to myself at any given moment in time. That "I" repeating throughout this citation, like the word "present" in my preface, works by undermining in each iteration the concept of a unified, self-present ego. Each repetition is a repetition with a difference, alerting the reader to an understanding that that "infinite difference" is not merely interpersonal, communal, and extrinsic. All worlds, at least all of Derrida's worlds, are queer unto themselves. They are bottomless, abyssal, unknowable—past the wit of man to say what dreams they are.

r

What is a responsible response in an act of reading? How can we know what a proper response would be like? Perhaps it is best to ask this question inversely. "So the non response. Clearly, it will always be possible to say, and it will be true, that non-response is a response. One always has, one always must have, the right not to respond, and this liberty belongs to responsibility itself, that is, to the liberty that one believes must be associated with it. One must always be free not to respond to an appeal or to invitation – and it is worth remembering this, to remind oneself of the essence of liberty" (Derrida 1992b, 15). What is the responsibility of the reader to the act of reading if one has also the freedom not to respond? If one can always say after Bartleby, "I prefer not to"? Reading will always incur a response. There is no nonresponse when one reads. Reading in that sense is a response to some demand being made on the reader by the text being read. But what happens in *Bartleby* is an allegory of what it might be like to not respond. "On the one hand the story demands to be read, with an authority like that of Bartleby himself over the narrator. Imperiously, imperatively, it says, 'Read me!' On the other hand it cannot be read. It demands an impossible task, and the reader remains paralyzed by the text, called upon to act but unable to act" (VP, 175). What is the most responsible response to Bartleby (*Bartleby*)? I prefer not to say.

I shirk the responsibility and cite Miller on the issue of undecidability in his latest book:

> The predicament manifests itself in a certain feeling of dissatisfaction in the critic. This small book on *Adam Bede* and *Middlemarch*

[*Reading for Our Time*], for example, necessarily mimes in one way, or another, whether I have wished to do so or not, this discomfort of reading. This happens both in the detail of comment on particular passages and in the overall order of my sections. If criticism is a parable of the act of reading, the displeasure of the text is a multiple dissatisfaction. It is the sense of having said too much and too little at the same time. The critic feels that there would always be something important more to say, even about a brief citation that has been discussed at length. I never quite get my formulations just right. I can never quite say everything that needs to be said, say it correctly, and have done with *Adam Bede* and *Middlemarch* (RT, 138).

The predicament of premature closure is endemic to literary criticism even when a critic takes responsibility, the most exigent responsibility imaginable, and does his level best to show you that what is happening exceeds the reading. So, the reading goes on again and again. The compulsion to write, and to write well, of any passage is the compulsion to have the right reading. Even though Miller claims that *Middlemarch* is essentially affirmative, he realizes the difficulties it poses. It is as true now as it ever was that we are all victims of misreading. As the narrator says of the hapless Casaubon in *Middlemarch*, "we all of us, grave or light, get our thoughts entangled in metaphors, and act fatally on the strength of them" (RT, 147). Whether we are like Casaubon seeking after a "Key to all Mythologies" or like Dorothea eventually aware of the futility of this search, the metaphors we live by undo reason and propel us toward chance and kings and dangerous men. We act as if our readings were justified by a higher authority, some rational beyond the play of metaphor. We seek authority outside of the reading. But the reality is that reading is often fatal. Just as Dorothea misread Casaubon, so did Casaubon misread his own written testaments. Though we are entangled in metaphors, we do make our own choices and those choices can have devastating consequences. Responsibility is necessarily impossible, but necessary nonetheless.

S

In Ernest Hemingway's short story "A Clean, Well-Lighted Place," two waiters engage in a puzzling conversation about an old man who sits drinking in the "shadow the leaves of the tree [make] against the electric light" (Oates 1992, 296).[25] The conversation amounts to a rather gossipy discussion about the old man's attempted suicide. As in all of Hemmingway's great stories, a simple premise depicted in simplistic and unadorned prose hints at something that cannot be quite put into words. The older of the two waiters is ostensibly understanding of the old man's wish to drink at the café late into the night, while the younger waiter merely wants the old man to finish his drink and leave so he can get back to his young wife. The old man eventually goes as does the young waiter shortly afterward, leaving the older waiter to continue the conversation with himself. Here are the final lines:

> It is the light of course but it is necessary that the place be clean and pleasant. You do not want music. Certainly you do not want music. Nor can you stand before a bar with dignity although that is

all that is provided for these hours. What did he fear? It was not fear or dread. It was a nothing he knew too well. It was all a nothing and a man was nothing too. It was only that and light was all it needed and a certain cleanness and order. Some lived in it and never felt it but he knew it all was nada y pues nada y nada y pues nada. Our nada who art in nada, nada be thy name thy kingdom nada thy will be nada in nada as it is in nada. Give us this nada our daily nada and nada us our nada as we nada our nadas and nada us into nada but deliver us from nada; pues nada. Hail nothing full of nothing, nothing is with thee. He smiled and stood before a bar with a shinning steam pressure coffee machine.

'What's yours?' asked the barman.

'Nada.'

'Otro loco mas,' said the barman and turned away.

'A little cup,' said the waiter.

The barman poured it for him.

'The light is very bright and pleasant but the bar is unpolished,' the
   waiter said.

The barman looked at him but didn't answer. It was too late at night
   for conversation.

'You want another copita?' the barman asked.

'No, thank you,' said the waiter and went out. He disliked bars and bodegas. A clean, well-lighted café was a very different thing. Now, without thinking further, he would go home to his room. He would lie in the bed and finally, with daylight, he would go to sleep. After all, he said to himself, it is probably only insomnia. Many must have it. (Oates 1992, 299–300)

I doubt many readers would agree with the waiter's diagnosis, though it is always possible that some may do so. "Insomnia" seems like another one of those nadas the waiter has been running idly through his mind. It functions like that rhetorical figure of understated speech known as litotes, as indeed we might say the entire story does. The waiters have simply been standing around their café discussing the attempted suicide of an old man who is obviously suffering from some acute form of depression, and yet they speak of the event in a euphemistic and rather blasé manner: "'Last week he tried to commit suicide,' one waiter said. 'Why?' 'He was in despair'" (296). But what is even more shocking than their apparent apathy is the way that the language of the text is working to create that apathy in the reader. Notice for instance the repetitions in the descriptions above. "You do not want music. Certainly you do not want music"; "What did he fear? It was not fear or dread." This is of course followed by all those nadas injected into the Our Father and Hail Mary, but only after the waiter has tried to define something. "It was" is repeated at the beginning of four consecutive sentences, while the word "it" continues to repeat throughout the passage. It was what? What was the "it"? It was nothing and yet that nothing was something.

That something is left unsaid, or rather *that* something is said in the repetitions of the words "nada" and "nothing." So the story is about nothing. And yet it is also about the possibility that the words "nothing" and "nada" speak of nothing in particular and therefore of some *thing*. When the words are repeated, they become emptied of their meaning. Each becomes what Miller calls a "surd": "A *surd* in mathematics is a sum containing one or more irrational roots of numbers. The square root of two is an irrational number. There is a square root of two, but it is not any number that can be said, rationally. A *surd* in phonetics is a voiceless sound, that is to say, a sound with no base in the vibration of the vocal chords. The original root of the word *surd, swer,* means to buzz or whisper . . . The Latin *surdus* was chosen in medieval mathematics to translate an Arabic term that was itself a translation of the Greek *alogos*: speechless, wordless, inexpressible, irrational, groundless" (LM, 394). Repeating a word over and over again, Miller also tells us in *Others*, is one way to see how a word can become a mere surd, how it can become "a sound emptied of meaning" (O, 246). You can try this, as he does and invites us to do, with your own name: Éamonn, Éamonn, Éamonn, Éamonn. Indeed, "Any word said over and over will ultimately be drained of meaning. We [therefore] all dwell on the borders of aphasia" (AT, 228).

"Nothing to be done," says Estragon at the beginning of Beckett's *Godot*, in a way that instigates a similar series of emptying nothings (Beckett 1985, 9). And as Vivien Mercier once famously said of it, it is a play in which "nothing happens twice."[26] "A Clean, Well-Lighted Place" is likewise a short story where nothing happens in two languages over and over again. Nada, nada y pues nada, nothing, nothing to be done. Translated back and forth between two languages, the languages speak of themselves, of their status as words. They are, therefore, I take it, examples of what de Man would refer to as the nonphenomenal materialism of language. Though what he means by this, Miller tells us, is not all that easy to get right. The easy way to explain this would be to say that language works on its own. But that does not quite hit the mark. It can also describe what language makes happen "before the mind starts 'reading'" (O, 246). The remarkable force of de Man's phrase is that it speaks of a being without idea, an absurd force in language that points to something other before the words are invested with meaning. If I am right, this is the meaning of Hemingway's story, or rather the way in which that text works to point to a meaningless meaning in the materiality of inscription. Beckett's Vladimir perhaps puts it best: "Words, words. (Pause.) Speak" (185, 50).

t

In his work on the question of writing about, on, or naming places, Miller pays close attention to the slippages inhabiting and circumscribing the word "topography": "Topography," we are told, "originally meant the creation of a metaphorical equivalent in words of a landscape. Then by another transfer, it came to mean representation of a landscape according to the conventional signs of some system of mapping. Finally, by a third transfer, the name of the map was carried over to name what it mapped" (T, 3). The latter meaning, he informs us, has far-reaching consequences for our reading of literature, since it subtly implies that the meanings of the words we use to name places, proper names like Sligo or Roscommon, Thor Ballylee or Howth Castle, are somehow, in a kind of Cratylism, innately descriptive or intrinsically linked to the places they describe. The idea is that by a unique figurative transfer each place-name carries with it a mimetic charge or trace phonetically or conceptually indicative of its origin. How difficult would it be for instance to think of a place nonlinguistically? Is it ever possible? Examples of this puzzling phenomenon abound in literature. Indeed, we might even say that literature is the best place to see how the confusion between a linguistic and a phenomenal reality takes place, so to speak.

In Hardy's *Jude the Obscure*, the novel which famously cured him of all compulsions to ever write another one, we see the young Jude Fawley (as his surname suggests) fall prey to a strange obsession. Jude has acquired an insatiable longing to better himself from the inspirational schoolmaster Richard Phillostson who's been describing the wonders of education to the impressionable young boy. Jude consequently longs to go to Christminster and experience for himself the wondrous atmosphere of a university town. After journeying out into distant fields, Jude climbs up a ladder onto a rooftop in order to glimpse the metropolis of his desires. This procedure then becomes a regular mode of escape for him, an opportunity to give way to his hopes of joining the scholars there:

> Through the solid barrier of cold cretaceous upland to the northward he was always beholding a gorgeous city–the fancied place he had likened to the New Jerusalem, though there was perhaps more of the painter's imagination, and less of the diamond merchant's in his dreams thereof than in those of the Apocalyptic writer. And the city acquired a tangibility, a permanence, a hold on his life, mainly from the one nucleus of fact that the man for whose knowledge and purposes he had so much reverence was actually living there; not only so, but living among the more thoughtful and mentally shining ones therein.
>
> In sad wet seasons, though he knew it must rain at Christminster too, he could hardly believe that it rained so drearily there. Whenever he could get away from the confines of the hamlet for an

hour or two, which was not often, he would steal off to the Brown
House on the hill and strain his eyes persistently; sometimes to be
rewarded by the sight of a dome or spire, at other times by a little
smoke, which in his estimate had some of the mysticism of incense.
(Hardy 1998, 18)

The remarkable thing about Jude's account of Christminster is that
it is mingled with the hopes and aspirations he has for that place.
Everything he thinks about in relation to it is charged with the
emotional yearning he has for the possibilities it can offer him as a
student. Christminster is an another world entirely. Marygreen, by
contrast, is sleepy and pastoral, a place of physical not mental toil, a
small farming village where nothing eventful seems to happen for the
boy. Christminster is closer to God's infinite wisdom and, ludicrously,
so Jude believes, protected from the rain at Marygreen. Even the
smoke is linked by metaphorical transfer from the distant cityscape to
the heavenly realm. The New Jerusalem of which he speaks is a clever
repetition of a suggestion made to him by a roof tiler a little earlier.
Jude, in short, takes the impressions others have of the place and
weaves a narrative around the name. Since he has no direct knowledge
of the city, he relies on the suggestiveness of that proper name to help
him: "Christ" means that the city is hallowed, whereas "minster" is
suggestive of its authority. The word "mynster" finds its roots in the
Old English term for a monastery and therefore also suggests Jude's
desire to become a servant to the higher scholastic orders there.

  Dickens' Pip famously performs a similar feat of interpretation
when reading the inscriptions on his late parents' tombstones in
the opening lines of *Great Expectations*: "The shape of the letters

on my father's [tombstone], gave me an odd idea that he was a square, stout, dark man, with curly black hair. From the character and turn of the inscription, '*Also Georgina Wife of the Above*', I drew a childish conclusion that my mother was freckled and sickly" (Dickens 1996, 3). Though Dickens' example is even more ludicrous than Hardy's, each one is an insightful comment on the dangers of misreading. Each example describes the foolhardiness of each of its protagonists and the force of their desires over their interpretations of the world. For both Jude and Pip, such misreadings will have dire consequences when both realize that they have invested their dreams in presumptions, preconceptions, and prejudices. Satis House, which for Pip had for so long been the floodgate of all of his fortune and passion, will become the scene of horrid remembrance, while Christminster, for Jude, will become the scene of the collapse of his university hopes.

The unsettling thing about these examples, however, is that they have a sinister message. Though each one condemns the childish reading, each makes it explicit that such readings are never avoidable, however attuned to these misreadings we become. You cannot *not* think of these words as somehow motivated: "Like all place names and proper names, in real life or in fiction," Miller says regarding another of Hardy's novels, "the names in *The Return of the Native* are somewhere on the scale between total arbitrariness and total motivation. A name wholly idiomatic, entirely 'proper,' altogether special to the person or place in question, would be idiotic, incomprehensible" (T, 46). All readings of place are, therefore, invariably misreadings in this way. They are readings which always work by association. Even my own list of proper place names is motivated in this way.

u

I proposed Steerforth's health. God bless him! . . . I broke my glass in going round the table to shake hands with him, and said (in two words) 'Steerforth – you'retheguidingstarofmyexist-ence.' . . . Somebody was smoking. We were all smoking. *I* was smoking, and trying to suppress a rising tendency to shudder . . . Somebody was leaning out of my bedroom window, refreshing his forehead against the cool stone of the parapet, and feeling the air upon his face. It was myself. I was addressing myself as 'Copperfield', and saying, 'why did you try to smoke? You might have known you couldn't do it.' . . . Somebody said to me, 'Let us go to the theatre, Copperfield!' . . . Owing to some confusion in the dark, the door was gone. I was feeling for it in the window-curtains, when Steerforth, laughing, took me by the arm and led me out. We went downstairs, one behind another. Near the bottom, somebody fell, and rolled down. Somebody else said it was Copperfield. I was angry at that false report, until, finding myself on my back in the passage, I began to think there might be some foundation for it (Dickens 1985, 420–2).

This witty passage from Dickens' *David Copperfield* is a wonderful example of anacoluthon and a somewhat metafictive ironic comment on the distance between the narrator and the author. Though our drunken protagonist is doubling his speech and mixing his pronouns in a laughably jubilant stupor, a result of his having hosted his first dinner party in his new London apartment, his sensations are in many ways analogous with Freud's notoriously indefinable concept of the uncanny, *das Unheimlich*.[27] Though the uncanny is less likely to manifest itself as a fearful or dreadful atmosphere in this section, given the passage's jocose rendering of the events of Copperfield's inebriated soiree, there is nonetheless a strange and uneasy mix of the horrid and the ridiculous, a commingling of the effects of doubling, repetition, déjà vu, a transposition of selves, dislocation of souls, within the same subject; there is in short a kind of *iter*ability where otherness and sameness are warring factions on the same side.

There is also an-other agency at work here at the level of the text, a conscience or super-ego working through the events of the evening in order to describe the illicit wanderings of the protagonist. This agency is of interest because it doubles the character and the narrator simultaneously by highlighting the distance between them on a literal and a fictive plane; it highlights a fissure between what structural narratologists such as Shlomith Rimmon-Kenan and Gérard Genette would refer to as the intradeigetic and extradeigetic strata of the text—a schism between a character within the text (Copperfield) and a character outside of the text (Copperfield's double self or super-ego). The uncanny doubling of the self within the narrative creates a ripple which crosses over the threshold of the inner and outer borders of the storyline, creating and disseminating the uneasy sense of repetition within the fictional world of the novel and the world outside.

It is as if the character is haunted by himself, that in order to tell his story and repeat his life in an ulterior narrative mode he must divide and double himself incessantly. In Schelling's famous formulation of this repetition, and in Freud's use of it, everything which should have remained hidden has suddenly come to light: the narrator, however frivolously, has created a parabasis in which the actual structure of the autobiography has ludicrously presented itself as a fictional account of a divided and invented self that can never be present to itself.[28] This narrative is, therefore, glimpsed as an ongoing schizophrenic and uncanny event or even advent. In the latter senses of which we could say that the atmosphere of the uncanny movement in the text transcends its momentary context and spreads throughout the entire novel, becoming a perpetual being-toward-death.

Copperfield, like Jane Eyre in Charlotte Brontë's (Currer Bell's) novel, is beside or rather outside himself.[29] The proliferation of "I"'s throughout the passages in this scene from *David Copperfield* interestingly reveals in each repetition a moving away from the unified subject as an ineluctable modality or Leibnizian monad. Each "I" reveals another character. One who smokes, one who stumbles, one who creates wonderful new neologisms—"you'retheguidingstarofmyexistence"—until finally we reach that zero point where "Somebody said to me, 'Let us go to the theatre, Copperfield!'". At which moment the "I" becomes so confused, so interchangeable, so diffuse, that it is impossible to figure out exactly who has just said this. "Somebody" and "I" have paradoxically become *Heimlich*, at home with each other in a reversal and repression of the "un" in the *Unheimlich*. Their secrets have surfaced. Each is the ghost of the other within the same. Each is the other other. And yet, this opening up onto the secret is something that must remain hidden or underneath the narrative if the story is to continue being a *Bildungsroman*, a progression toward the maturity of one-self. Who asks Copperfield to go to the theatre? You, I, he, she does, and all together and all at once, at the very same moment in the act of reading. The "I" allows for all of these possibilities because it is other to itself and the self-same at once. "I" cannot in fact say I.

"I" only ever perform I through a promise made to myself and to others to remain faithful to an ideality. I do this in every act of signature and countersignature, every reiteration of the proper name which is never truly proper; "I" do this in memory of me: "Even the secret regions of the silent self are divided by the iterability of the mark" (SA, 110).

Separating what he calls the canny from the uncanny critics in "Stevens' Rock and Criticism as Cure, II," Miller makes a distinction between critics who tend toward a more schematic or scientific criticism, such as Todorov, Jakobson, and Genette, and those uncanny critics whose view is not so much less scientific or rigorous in its attention to the text as open to the possibility that there will always be more to say (TNT, 117–31). Echoing Stevens, Miller suggests that the uncanny critic gets to a point where the work (the criticism or primary text) "resists the intelligence almost successfully," a point where logic fails and insight, in effect, begins. The paradoxical "insight" of the essay is that the necessary blindness in reading, the "abyssing" or alogical grounding of criticism, becomes again a mode of insight. Thus, like Freud's ambivalent etymological rendering of the *Heimlich/Unheimlich* distinction, the canny becomes uncanny and the uncanny canny. The distinction, like the singularity and iterability of the "I" or "as if," "comme si," of fictional discourse is a problem that can never be simply overcome by appeals to some ultimate binarity between the imaginary and the real as Freud had already to some extent realized.[30] The perpetual danger of entrapment is figured at the point where the "I" becomes either canny or uncanny. Like Ariadne's Labyrinth, all texts, no matter how linear, logical, or logocentric, share something of the uncanny, an admixture of the two, since, as Dickens adequately shows us, the subject is itself the uncanny ground of criticism.

V

In *On Literature*, Miller refers to an aporia in reading, which he identifies with the musicological terminology for slow and fast movements in a piece of music: *lento* and *allegro*. In the latter tempo, the reader gives him- or herself over to what Miller following Kant calls "Schwärmerei." "Schwärmerei" names that process of creating a virtual reality when we read a given literary text. The way we enthusiastically give ourselves over to a kind of madness. The word "allegro" in Italian is also suggestive of the joy experienced in this process as well as the speed at which it happens to us. Moreover, reading as "Schwärmerei" is by no means a passive act, since any reading requires an effort on the behalf of the reader, an active participation. For Kant in the third part of the *Critique of Pure Reason*, this manner of suspending disbelief is a kind of stupidity, and, worse, a dangerous irrationalism. The critical faculties must always be deeply suspicious of the irrational or nonrational.

Miller's argument in *On Literature*, however, is that this process is in some sense a natural and necessary part of reading literature. In order to experience a novel as a story, we must be able to read quickly and allow ourselves to be taken in by what happens in the work. We have to, in other words, be willing to commit (an active verb here) to the way the words impress upon us the possibilities of an alternate world. "One must," he says, "give all one's faculties to re-creating the work's imaginary world as fully and as vividly as possible within oneself. For those who are no longer children, or childlike, a different kind of effort is necessary too. This is the attempt, an attempt that may well not succeed, to suspend ingrained habits of 'critical' or suspicious reading . . . You must become as a little child if you are to read literature rightly" (OL, 120). The flipside to the aporia is that one must also learn to read lento (slowly) in order to produce "good" readings. "Slow reading, critical reading, means being suspicious at every turn, interrogating every detail of the work, trying to figure out by just what means the magic is wrought" (OL, 122). The aporia is the law that says in order to read literature correctly you must be able to read as a naïve *and* an experienced reader at once. This kind of reading is impossible but exists as a demand made by any novel we may choose to read: "I meant it when I said you must read in both ways at once, impossibly" (OL, 156).

The major example running throughout and embracing *On Literature* is *The Swiss Family Robinson*, a book Miller read at the age of ten. This book, he claims, is a "marvellous allegory" for what happens in the event of virtuality. Something new is created by "hard work and ingenuity," a "new realm," just as "New Switzerland" was created by the family on a remote island somewhere in the East Indies. But 65 years on, and after a lifetime of literary study and critical reading, the story manifests another agenda. It is "unashamedly patriarchal and sexist"; it posits a Protestant ethic of "family values" against the self-reliance manifested in its precursor text *Robinson Crusoe*; and it propagates an imperialist propaganda not easily identifiable by a 10-year-old enchanted by life in the wilderness. Like Elizabeth Förster-Nietzsche's attempted settlement in Papua New Guinea, which was to be called "New Germany" by the way, Wyss's "New Switzerland" smacks of an aggressive imperialist ideology and aspiring cultural hegemony.

The Swiss Family Robinson at any rate *seems*, as children's books often do, to be naïve and unreflective, beyond ideology. Much of its allure, despite its implicit ideological underpinnings, is that this virtual world is easily entered into and will reward the effort with adventure and a new understanding of the world around us. Even survival skills, as Miller humorously points out in his continuing belief that he might, if need be, be able to survive on an island, given the experience of having read the book, form a charming example of how deeply these works can affect us and remain in our unconscious. I take a counterexample here though to show how I think the reverse affect may also be encountered in reading. This time from Nabokov's *Lolita*:

> She had entered my world, umber and black Humberland, with rash curiosity; she surveyed it with a shrug of amused distaste; and it seemed to me now that she was ready to turn away from it with something akin to plain repulsion. Never did she vibrate under my touch, and a strident 'what d'you think you are doing?' was all I got for my pains. To the wonderland I had to offer, my fool preferred the corniest movies, the most cloying fudge. To think that between a Hamburger and a Humburger, she would—invariably, with icy precision—plump for the former. Did I mention the name of that milk bar I visited a moment ago? It was, of all things, The Frigid Queen. Smiling a little sadly, I dubbed her My Frigid Princess. She did not see the wistful joke.
>
> Oh, do not scowl at me reader, I do not intend to convey the impression that I did not manage to be happy. Reader must understand that in the possession and thraldom of a nymphet the

enchanted traveller stands, as it were, *beyond happiness*. (Nabokov 1960, 163) [original emphasis]

I've chosen this example to show how the naïve reading can be turned on its head so to speak. If Miller is right, and I believe he is, that good reading must be naïve as well as critical, and that this entails an aporetic experience, I can think of no better example than Nabokov's diabolical tale of sexual misconduct to show how dangerous a naïve reading can be and how impossible in this case.

Lolita is about as far away from *The Swiss Family Robinson* as it is possible to get. A confessional written hastily by a man with an insatiable lust for pubescent girls before his trial for murder, the novel is explicitly an ironic indictment of childish naivety. But not only in the sense that Lolita herself, a jejune 12-year old, is being duped by an unscrupulous deviant. It is also, I would argue, a critical reflection on the aporia of reading *lento* and *allegro*. One of Nabokov's first published works was a translation of *Alice in Wonderland* into Russian.[31] And this passage positively teems with Carrollian overtones. Nabokov's Alice has entered a dark and shadowy underworld. The word "umber" used to form the protagonist's name, "Humbert," or "Hummy" as he affectionately refers to himself when he marries Lolita's mother Charlotte ("Hummy and mummy"), means shady or shadowy, from the Italian word "*ombra*" (shadow) or the Latin word "*umbra*" (shade). It can also interestingly refer to the visor of a helmet, something which hides the face. Lolita's "Wonderland" has here become "Humberland." Her rabbit-hole has led to a very dark place indeed, a place she cannot possibly see through or fully understand. The references to the Frigid Queen, as well as the witty word-play, are also Carrollian in scope.

But what is even more frightening about the passage, as indeed one might say the book itself, is that the reader often finds him- or herself drawn into identifying with Humbert on a naïve level. Humbert's ("Hummy's) wry wit and bristling linguistic humor is describing the journey Lolita has taken from naivety to experience and in doing so is producing an allegory of virtual automobility.[32] The journey Lolita takes, in other words, is also describing the journey the reader of the novel takes from the real world to umber Humberland. What is ordinarily a voyage from "rash curiosity" to "plain repulsion" is foregrounded by the narrator's wistful desire to keep the reader in thraldom, to keep the reader preferring the Humburger.

The final lines are an exquisite plea to his audience to remain naïve and suspend disbelief: "Oh, do not scowl at me, reader, I do not intend to convey the impression that I did not manage to be happy. Reader must understand that in the possession and thraldom of a nymphet the enchanted traveller stands, as it were, *beyond happiness*." The omission of syntax in the second line, "Reader must understand" is the kind of thing people often do when speaking to children. A naivety is required to be taken in by it and a quick reading will easily miss the artifice employed to make this happen, as the jocose punning becomes a salient and entrancing part of the narrative drowning it out. Another word for what the "enchanted traveller" finds "beyond happiness" might be "Schwärmerei," a maddening delusion beyond reason and objectivity. This is precisely what *Lolita* does as a novel. It makes it easy for the reader to read naively; it encourages it. But it also makes us stop short at various intervals, by telling us that the naïve reading is abhorrent. What this doubling force does, in short, is create the most disturbingly likeable virtual reality by inviting its readers to read both ways impossibly.

W

"As we read we compose, without thinking about it, a kind of running commentary or marginal jotting that adds more words to the words on the page. There is always already writing as the accompaniment to reading" (TNT, 301). Miller calls this "first writing." It is what we do when we are silently writing on our own mystic writing pads, to employ a Freudian metaphor, the words of the pages we read. Those words are automatically inscribed on the palimpsest of the mind, if you will, where all the readings we have performed have been and gone before. All reading in this sense is a kind of writing that appropriates what is in the work to a rationalizing consciousness, as in the way the random access memory of a computer works to store retrievable memory. In this way, the meaning of the work is acquired, reaped from the page. This primary writing, which Miller describes in the *MLA Newsletter*, is the kind of writing that manifests itself in the scholarly essays published in books or literary journals, what becomes "part of that vast enterprise of rationalizing appropriation, of making regular, comprehensible, usable, familiar, ready for the archives that is the essence of the modern research university" (TNT, 301).

For Miller, the "first writing" is a response to what the work itself responded to, not a response to the strangeness of the work itself. "Secondary" writing is more rigorous still, or less so, depending on how one envisages the responsible response to a kind of excessive encounter in the act of writing. "Mixed with the apotropaic act of covering over in 'the first writing,' scribbled so to speak in invisible ink in the margin of the book we read, there is something else, a submission to what the work itself submitted to. This submission dispossess the reader, appropriates him or her, rather than yielding itself to rationalizing appropriation. It too carries over into the essay, chapter or review, in spite of our best efforts to conceal it. Such carrying over gives, perhaps, the chief interest and value to what to write" (TNT, 302). Writing we might say is then a response to something occurring in the readings we make: first as a response to the writings we unconsciously make in the margins of the text, our hermeneutic impulse, and then to something that supposes that writing as it appears through the work. One word for what that secondary element is, or, better, might be, is otherness.

What is always excessive in any act of writing is what remains after everything the primary writing says has been said. There is always something unquantifiable in any reading, that which demands further reading and writing. James, we are told, refers to this in his writings as the "matter" or "thing." What Miller calls "the two kinds of secondary reading" are the ways in which the responses to what is strange about the primary writing can be either attempts to "cover over" what is idiomatic or eccentric or attempts to "remain faithful" to that eccentricity. The uneasy vacillating condition of this experience is known as unreadability: "Unreadability is the generation by the text itself of a desire for the possession of a single meaning, while at the same time the text itself frustrates this desire" (RN, 98). The more responsive one becomes in one's own readings to this condition, the more, paradoxically, one will feel the need to write. This is the demand reading-writing places always already on our shoulders. "Between conduct in the ordinary sense and the act of writing there are differences but no separations" (ER, 103). If reading is nowhere finalized, then writing, likewise, cannot *not* be performed. Whether we do so in the margins of the texts we read or in scholarly essays or books, writing like reading goes on, excessively. Miller's writing is, therefore, like Derrida's or de Man's, or indeed any other good reader's, a kind of general economy. "It is the mode of excessive production which cannot be accounted for by the desire for meaning which informs hermeneutic reading practices, and which leaves in its wake excessive traces" (Wolfreys 1998b, 6). It is also of course, and because of this, unlike any of these. Singular. Unique. Idiomatic. Excessive.

X

For Geoffrey Bennington

X marks the spot. Like the cross-hairs in the telescopic sight, the intersection of the lines marking the point to aim at.

X crosses through, does the *sous rature*, leaving legible what it simultaneously cancels, for example the words 'is' and 'thing' in a famous sentence of Derrida's.

X is the chiasmus, where lines meet at a point and continue, never to meet again, the *quadrifurcum* that will have organized so much of Derrida's writing, the *chi* that drives the reading of Adami's fish-picture, the fish dragged from its element only to fall back in, that will have given me my favourite pedagogical support for the explanation of the quasi-transcendental.

X is forbidden, and therefore desirable, censored, and therefore uncensorable.

X shows which dotted line I have to sign.

I imagine X as a three-dimensional representation: of a pyramid seen from above, rising to its definite point, or of a rectangular shaft disappearing into the infinite depths, the central point a mere perspectival vanishing never arrived at, however long the fall. (Bennington 2000a, 76)

X is everything and nothing. A quasi-transcendental. It is the mystery of what is there and not there, Nietzsche's "mysterious X" [*das rätselhafte X*] (LM, 330; T, 179). X brings two poles together and separates them. It is a figure for metaphor, for kissing, for Christ, for crossroads, for the male chromosome, for no parking, for an illustration, and so on and so forth. X for Miller is all of these things together, the figure of the labyrinth in narrative and the linguistic moment. "The real and the unreal, the metaphorical and the literal, the figure and the ground, constantly change places, in oscillating chiasmus, for 'ex'ample in Stevens's contradictory explanation of 'sea of ex' in his letters" (AT, 25).

y

"'To spin yarns' is a cliché for narration," says Miller in one of his many readings of *Heart of Darkness*. "To tell a story is to join many threads together to make a continuous line leading from here to there. Of that yarn cloth may be woven, the whole cloth of the truth as opposed to a lie that, as the proverbial saying has it, is 'made up out of whole cloth'. The lie as cloth makes a web, screen, or veil covering a truth that remains hidden behind or within" (O, 124). The figure of the yarn for storytelling comes to Miller via the following oft-quoted lines from the novel:

> The yarns of seamen have a direct simplicity, the whole meaning of which lies within the shell of a cracked nut. But Marlow was not typical (if his propensity to spin yarns be excepted), and to him the meaning of an episode was not like a kernel but outside [the ms has 'outside in the unseen'], enveloping the tale which brought it out only as a glow brings out a haze, in the likeness of one of those misty halos that sometimes are made visible by the spectral illumination of moonshine. (O, 20; TPP, 182; FR, 26)[33]

Here, the figure describes the relationship between what is inside and outside of the story. Most sailors tell stories in such a way that the meaning is detachable, appropriable outside of the story itself, and able to be passed on to others in a different way when it is retold and reformulated again. The story can be rewoven, if you will, spun into a different pattern without its kernel being affected. Marlow's story on the other hand is not reappropriable in quite the same way as the stories told by other sailors. The kernel of his story is on the outside, in the appearance or way it is told. The figure moves the reader from asking questions like "what is the meaning of the story?" "what is its point?" to questions like "how does the story work?" The shift from the "what" to the "how" of meaning is instrumental because it allows the reader to catch a glimpse of something not ordinarily glimpsed in the act of reading. Instead of searching for an ultimate meaning, something that will allow all of the parts of the story hang together, so to speak, a general formulation such as Marlow's story is about the search for, and the ultimate discovery of, a strange figure called Kurtz; the story more properly embodies the possibility that all stories are about the impossibility of weaving the final yarn. The paradox is that there is no outside of yarning, no beyond the warp and woof of storytelling, and yet all yarns are excuses (another meaning of the word "yarn") for not being able to certify their meanings. Pardon for not meaning.[34] Conrad makes the darkness visible, by showing us that the secret is all on the surface: "There was nothing either above or below him, and I knew it" (Conrad 1995, 170).

Z

Zero Plus One brings us back to the present, loops us back like the J. in J. Hillis Miller, or the J. in John, as Derrida used to call him.[35] Zero is an odd number for J. Hillis Miller. It both is and is not a number. Each time we begin to speak of zero, the paradox of is and is not, the simultaneity of presence and absence in a single figure, becomes an issue that refuses to be settled in a definitive fashion: "There can be no *one* without zero, but the zero always appears in the guise of a *one*, of (some)thing. The name is the trope of the zero. The zero is always *called* a one, when the zero is actually nameless, 'innomable'. 'One' is straightforwardly and intelligibly both a number and not a number. Zero, however, is unnameable" (ZO, 87). The question then is how can one ever get from zero to one or from one back to zero? How can one ever move in such a radically nihilistic aporia? I've called this a "nihilistic aporia" because it is a question, as arguably it always is with Miller, about how something comes from nothing, a return to Parmenides' fundamental proposition: *Nihil ex nihilo fit.* But is this really nihilism in the relativistic sense critics of Miller's work from Wayne Booth to M. H. Abrams to Frank Lentricchia have seen in it? Not if we recognize in this an experience of the impossible that ironically makes the impossible possible in Derridean parlance. "The exhaustion of thematics, of semantic import, does not leave mere emptiness: as Miller so elegantly demonstrates, zero is a number after all, albeit one which challenges the foundation of number" (Attridge 2004, 120).

There is a nothing that is not there and a nothing that is for the listener in Stevens's poem "The Snow Man," a nothing that one must have "a mind of winter" to behold. This nothingness is nameless and silent. The listener "nothing himself beholds" (Stevens 1990, 10). But of course he beholds some(thing). That "thing" of which the poet cannot speak is given many names in literature; zero being one of them. The name is the trope of the zero because it catachrestically calls that nothing a something and in the process covers over the gap between being and nonbeing. Likewise, the leaps of knowing and not knowing in acts of reading are covered over by naming the event and forming a line. Each time there is a movement from a to b, the same paradox is arguably at issue. Readers form a line where there is none. They fill in the gaps. The most concise formulation of this comes from Yeats in "Adam's Curse":

A line will take us hours maybe;

Yet if it does not seem a moment's thought,

Our stitching and unstitching has been naught.

(Yeats 1966, 204)

In order to get from zero to one or from a to b, the author and reader *must* cover over the gaps; they must forget that they are passing over a paradox. Miller simply brings this to light. He shows us that the stitching has indeed been naught, or rather naught plus one.

Notes

1   Peggy Kamuf, "Composition Displacement," *MLN* 121.4 (2006), 872–92, p. 887.

2   For more on this, see Jacques Derrida's fascinating essay on Hillis Miller and Paul de Man, "'Le Parjure,' *Perhaps*: Storytelling and Lying ('abrupt breaches in syntax')" in *Without Alibi* (Stanford: Stanford University Press, 2002). Though this essay is a celebration of the work of Hillis Miller, Derrida, rightfully to my mind, rejects his essay's place in the genre of "text in homage." The reading Derrida is undertaking here is a following (a paradoxical approach) of anacoluthon in Miller's texts, referring to it as "doubtless more than a figure of rhetoric, despite appearances, it signals in any case toward the *beyond* of rhetoric *within* rhetoric" (167). Derrida's key point is that in order to do a kind of justice to Miller's work, rather than simply pay homage, which he also does by the way, he must really "read" Miller. Toying with the etymology of the word "anacoluthon," Derrida comes upon the "acolyte" and questions the relationship between the line he feels he must take through the work of Miller and the notion of the active reading. "In a structural and regular fashion," he says, "the acolyte takes on, as we will verify, an anacolytic figure" (181). Aside from the subtle joke involved in this "we," a joke which persists throughout the essay, Derrida's argument is crucial to a thinking through of the idea of a critical distance in reading—there is no such thing, if "we" are conscious that there is nothing distant about criticism in the first place—and a responsible response. This book takes as its own *raison d'etre* a stake in what Derrida is saying here

of the act of reading as a responsible response to the text of Miller. By
realizing that Miller is a reader-at-work in the texts he criticizes, Derrida
involves himself in a rereading, which is also an "auseinandersetzung," of
Miller reading Proust as well as Proust reading Miller. In short, Derrida
must reinvent that responsibility of inventive reading through both Miller
and Proust in order to do some kind of justice to the acts of reading being
performed at such a high level of critical awareness: "with a gesture whose
necessity and elegance I have always admired," says Derrida, "it is in the
text of Proust himself that Miller finds what he *invents*: namely, a noun
and a concept that he will then put to work in a productive, demonstrative,
generalizable, fashion – well beyond this unique literary root, well beyond
this *oeuvre* . . . I believe I must prefer here the word 'invention' because it
hesitates perhaps, it is suspended undecidably between *creative* invention,
the production of what is not – or was not earlier – and *revelatory*
invention, the discovery and unveiling of what *already* is or finds itself to be
there. Such an invention thus hesitates *perhaps*, it is suspended undecidably
between fiction and truth, but also between lying and veracity, that is,
between truth and fidelity" (WA, 167–8). If Miller's work is to be read,
really read in the sense by which he uses this word, then such readings must
resist that passive osmotic path of paraphrastic celebration in favor of an
active re-invention and recreation of that *perhaps* which led him to the text
in the first place—there is surely something proleptically democratic in this.
There will be more to say about these topics below.

3 For Miller's very positive review of Said's *Beginnings: Intention and
Method*, "Beginning with a Text," see *Theory and Now and Then*,
pp. 133–42. Here, Miller postulates that such a courageous, intelligent, and
insightful piece of scholarship suggests a way "beyond deconstruction"
without forgetting its insights. In his preface to the 1985 edition of his
book, Said acknowledges the importance of Miller's work as a rigorous
attentiveness to rhetoric and language but distances himself from the
kind of "uncanny criticism" envisioned in the review. A closer look at
this rather cheerful rebuttal from Said leads one into interesting territory:
what differences are there between Miller and Said on the question of
history? One suspects that Said senses a little too much of what he refers
to here as "the New New Criticism" in Miller—a very different way of
viewing the relation between textual analysis and sociopolitical and
epistemonarratological histories.

4 See *Reading Narrative*, pp. 47–9: "Narratology – the word means
the knowledge or science of narrative. This present book, in its
demonstration that this knowledge is not possible, might be called a
work of ananaratology." See also Dan Shen's even-handed discussion of

the complementary intersection of narratological and ananarratological arguments in Miller's work in *Provocations to Reading: J Hillis Miller and the Democracy to Come*, pp. 14–29. Here, she argues that rather than being simply antagonistic to structural narratological issues, Miller's work "broadens the horizon of narratological investigation."

5 See Nicholas Royle's interview with Julian Wolfreys, "The Beginning Is Haunted: Teaching and the Uncanny" in *Thinking Difference: Critics in Conversation* (New York: Fordham, 2004); and *The Uncanny* (Manchester: Manchester University Press, 2003b): "The uncanny entails another thinking of beginning: the beginning is already haunted," p. 1. It is divided within itself and harbors the residual hanging-over, in Derridean terminology, of the ghost of the undecidable. The beginning is haunted by this anxiety and remains always in this uneasy state of tension.

6 See Derrida's remarkable "Aphorism Countertime" in Derek Attridge, ed., *Jacques Derrida: Acts of Literature* (London: Routledge, 1992a), pp. 414–33. Here, Derrida speaks of the name in Shakespeare's *Romeo and Juliet*, and of the aphorism as being *a contretemps*, out of joint or out of time in a more musical sense. Beginnings, he says here, are out time, and in a remarkable phrase he refers to aphorisms as "the alea of an initial anachrony." The aphorism, a fragment of discourse cut off from the narrative form, he muses, is, "despite appearances . . . part of a serial logic," but a logic given over to chance. We should be able to infer from this that beginnings are, therefore, always a question of chance and sequentiality. One could perhaps argue that O'Brien's oeuvre is even working on the aleatory ground of a "third-time lucky" superstition.

7 Siegfried Sassoon "In Me, Past, Present, Future Meet" in Sir Arthur Quiller-Couch, ed., *The Oxford Book of English Verse 1250–1918* (Oxford: Oxford University Press, 1943b), p. 1133.

8 W. B. Yeats "A Dialogue of Self and Soul" in Peter Allt and Russell K. Alspach, eds, *The Variorum Edition of the Poems* (London: Macmillan, 1966), pp. 477–9.

9 For specific discussions on the subject of decision by Miller, see the following: "Who or What Decides, for Derrida: A Catastrophic Theory of Decision" in *For Derrida* (New York: Fordham, 2009); "What is a Kiss? Isabel's Moments of Decision," *Critical Inquiry*, Spring 2005, pp. 722–46; "Moments of Decision in *Bleak House*" in *The Cambridge Companion to Dickens* (Cambridge: Cambridge University Press, 2001), pp. 49–63; "'Taking up a Task': Moments of Decision in Ernesto Laclau's Thought" in Simon Critchley and Oliver Marchart, ed., *Laclau: A Critical Reader*

(London: Routledge, 2004), pp. 217–25; "The Degree Zero of Criticism" in Julian Wolfreys, ed., *Thinking Otherwise: Critics in Conversation* (New York: Fordham, 2004), pp. 147–64, and, see also, "On Literature and Ethics: An Interview with J Hillis Miller" in *The European English Messenger*, 15.1, 2006, pp. 23–34. Here, Miller very lucidly and pointedly discusses his reading of Derrida's theories of decision in relation to his own.

10 In the essay referenced in note 15 below, Miller says of decision "people do not usually, in ordinary language, say, 'I decide'. They say, 'I have decided'. That suggests that the decision is taken as an inward and spiritual act of conscience that is then later on reported, constatively, by saying, 'I want you all to know that I have decided,'" pp. 3–4.

11 Some of the following lines have also appeared in an essay entitled "Finding What You Want in Paul Auster's City of Glass" in Bárbara Arizti and Silvia Martínez-Falquina, eds, *On the Turn: The Ethics of Fiction in Contemporary Narrative in English* (Cambridge: Cambridge Scholars Press, 2007), pp. 400–14. I thank the editors for their kind permission to reproduce these lines from my earlier essay here.

12 See Brian McHale's, *Postmodernist Fiction* (London: Routledge, 2001), pp. 3–25. Here, McHale argues that a change in "dominant" points to one way of noticing the differences between Modernist and Postmodernist fiction: "This in a nutshell is the function of the dominant: it specifies the *order* in which different aspects are to be attended to, so that, although it would be perfectly possible to interrogate a postmodernist text about its epistemological implications, it is more *urgent* to interrogate it about its ontological implications. In postmodernist texts, in other words, epistemology is *backgrounded*, as the price for foregrounding ontology," p. 11. McHale sounds understandably uneasy about offering denominations in such passages.

13 See also Chapter 2 of *For Derrida* "Who or What Decides: For Jacques Derrida; A Catastrophic Theory of Decision," pp. 9–27. Here, Miller distinguishes between three aporias of decision in Derrida's "Force de loi; Le 'Fondement mystique de l'autoritié.'" First aporia: "*L'épokhē de la règle*" (épokhē of the rule). Using the Husserlian word for suspension, Derrida argues that a decision, to be a just decision, must be both free and not free in the sense that it must respond both to the singularity of any given situation and not deviate wildly from the law. Here, Miller, quoting Derrida, says "In Derrida's case [and I have decided that this is Hillis Miller's own view of the matter also], the justice or not of a given moment of decision can never be known. 'It follows from this paradox', he [Derrida] says, 'that

there is never a moment that we can say *in the present* that a decision *is* just (i.e., free and responsible), or that someone *is* a just man – even less, '*I am just*'. Justice is not a matter of is or of the present." Second aporia: "the ghost of the undecidable" or "La hantise de l'indécidable" (the haunting of the undecidable). What Derrida calls "an impossible decision," one that passes through the conflict of the undecidable ("two equally compelling obligations") and must be made urgently, is haunted by a conflict which must be exorcized at the moment of deciding. Here, Derrida talks of the call from the wholly other which bears down upon the impossible decision as an obligation to something unknowable and at the time compelling. This something other or some other other incites from an infinite place or idea of justice, which Derrida has at times called undeconstructible. On this latter point, Miller differs somewhat from Derrida, as he confesses that he does not hear "that still small voice" making a demand on him [see my *J. Hillis Miller and the Possibilities of Reading*, p. 131]. Miller notices in this reading that Derrida distinguishes between the event and decision: "The undecidable that presides over the non-phenomenal moment of decision is a kind of ghost, neither present nor not present, neither embodied nor wholly disembodied. It haunts and undermines the whole temporal process of decision. The result is that one can never speak of a decision as an 'event.'" Third aporia: "the urgency that obstructs the horizon of knowledge." Here, Derrida speaks of the urgency of decision and the feeling that it is something that happens to you, or seems to come from a different place. "The madness of decision derives from the fact that it is not the result of a conscious deliberation on the part of the decider, but something that happens to him or her, something he or she passively endures, as though the decision were made somewhere else, as though it came from the other." The crux of the argument is that this passivity to the incoming of the other is not an excuse for doing nothing but a realization of the complexity and necessity of really thinking about the consequences of our decisions and the responsibilities we have to others in making them. Miller, referring to the catastrophic nature of the Derridean theory of decision-making, is conscious of the incalculability of performative utterances here, as he is in his discussions of decisions in literature, which is one way of seeing how the most innocent choice can result in the most aberrant and perverse consequences.

14 See Geoffrey Bennington's "Inter" in Martin McQuillan, Graeme MacDonald, Robin Purves, and Stephen Thomson, eds, *Post-Theory: New Directions in Theory* (Edinburgh: Edinburgh University Press, 2000a), pp. 103–22.

15 See for instance Miller's discussions of de Man in *Speech Acts in Literature*, *The Ethics of Reading*, and especially "'Reading' Part of a Paragraph in *Allegories of Reading*" in *Theory Now and Then*, where Miller chooses this example.

16 For more on Wellerisms, see Wolfgang Meider and Stewart A. Kingsbury, eds, *A Dictionary of Wellerisms* (Oxford: Oxford University Press, 1994).

17 See the Choose Your Own Adventure website on http://www.cyoa.com/ (accessed 29/10/12). I am quoting here from R. A. Montgomery's *The Abominable Snowman* (1979), No. 1 in the series, which can be accessed partially on the website. Each one of the 184 titles begins with a similar warning. What I feel is interesting about this website is the fact that as a child I experienced these novels as already hypertextual and therefore their interactive web form is strangely in agreement with how I first read them years ago, before I was introduced to the internet. The hyperlinks, that is, are still an oddly familiar part of the experience of reading those books for the very first time. The popularity of the series (250 million books in print in 38 languages) is surely indicative of the excitement children experience in choosing their own way through these stories, though of course those choices are structurally manufactured; for example, there are 28 separate endings for *The Abominable Snowman*. The website also informs me that in 2006 an iPod version of *The Abominable Snowman* was released using the "Notes" function that allowed for hyperlink capabilities. These novels, therefore, not only intensify the question of decision in reading, but also now pose all sorts of interesting questions concerning the disparities between printed and digitized literature. Though the choices the reader can make in his or her reading may be calculable in a practical sense (28 endings), they are not calculable at a fundamental level where readers knowingly or unknowingly are choosing all the time.

18 For Miller's discussions of what Maurice Blanchot calls an "unavowable community," and what Jean-Luc Nancy would call an "unworked community," see Chapter 3 of *Literature as Conduct*, "Unworked and Unavowable: Community in *The Awkward Age*"; "The Indigene and the Cybersurfer" in *Ariel*, vol. 34, no. 1 (January 2003); and, especially, Chapter 1 of *The Conflagration of Community: Fiction Before and After Auschwitz*, "Nancy Contra Stevens."

19 I think here of course of Nietzsche's relationship with Emerson, two early practitioners of the joyful science. In *Twilight of the Idols*, Nietzsche famously refers to Emerson in the following exuberantly reverential vein: "Such a man as instinctively feeds on pure ambrosia and leaves alone the

indigestible in things . . . Emerson possess that good-natured and quick-
witted cheerfulness that discourages all earnestness; he has absolutely
no idea how old he is or how young he will be – he could say of himself,
in the words of Lope de Vega: '*yo me sucedo a mi mismo*' [I am my own
successor]. His spirit is always finding reasons for being contented and
grateful; and now and then he verges on the cheerful transcendence of
that worthy gentleman who, returning from an amorphous rendezvous
tamquam re bene gesta [as if things had gone well], said gratefully: '*Ut desint
vires, tamen est laudanda voluptas*' [Though the power be lacking, the lust
is praiseworthy]" (86). Miller has commented on this, via the relationship
between Emerson, Nietzsche, and Carlyle, in his "'Hieroglyphical Truth'
in *Sartor Resartus*: Carlyle and the Language of Parable" in *Victorian
Subjects*, pp. 303–19. For the best single text on the relationship between
these writers, see George J. Stack's excellent *Nietzsche and Emerson: An
Elective Affinity* (Athens: Ohio University Press, 1992). Here, Stack suggests,
"Philosophy is not an end in itself. It ought, ideally, to enhance life. Beyond
reflection, beyond ratiocination, beyond theories, beyond interpretations
lies a goal that can be discerned in the interstices of the texts of Emerson
and Nietzsche: *ekstasis*" (ix). Another word for this would be joy or, as
Juliet Flower MacCannell argues convincingly in *Provocations to Reading*,
"*jouissance*," pp. 3–14.

20 See for example Chapter 2 of *Literature as Conduct*, "The Story of a Kiss:
Isabel's Decision in The Portrait of a Lady," pp. 30–83; the Preface to
Zero Plus One and of course "Thomas Hardy, Jacques Derrida, and the
'Dislocation of Souls,'" in *Tropes, Parables, Performatives*, pp. 171–80.

21 I owe this thinking to a remarkable paper delivered by Nicholas Royle at
the "Derrida and Queer Theory" conference at University College Dublin
on 25th of July 2007. In his paper, entitled "Impossible Uncanniness," Royle
discussed what he called the "queer time" of deconstruction via Freud's
Nachträglichkeit and Derrida's reading of Miller in the essay "Justices."
This paper has since been republished as "Impossible Uncanniness:
Deconstruction and Queer Theory" in his *In Memory of Jacques Derrida*
(Edinburgh: Edinburgh University Press, 2009), pp. 113–33.

22 For a good explanation of how de Man's parodic formulation of speech acts
actually generate history or are historical events, see Miller's "Promises,
Promises: Speech Act Theory, Literary Theory, and Politico-Economic
Theory in Marx and de Man" in *NLH*, vol. 33, no. 1 (Winter 2002), pp. 1–20.

23 See also Miller's discussion of Hopkins in *The Linguistic Moment*,
pp. 229–66: "If he speaks adequately of his self-taste, he will, like Nimrod,

speak a private language and so communicate nothing: Raphel maì amècche zabì almi," p. 245. The latter sentence is taken from Dante's *Inferno* Canto XXXI, in which it is said of Nimrod that he speaks gibberish.

24 I owe this example to an intriguing paper I heard Nicholas Royle deliver at the *Critical Consciousness II* conference, "HélèneCixous and Jacques Derrida: Their Psychoanalyses," at the University of Leeds, 3 June 2007.

25 For the best essay on this short story, see David Lodge's *The Novelist at the Crossroads and Other Essays on Fiction and Criticism* (Ithaca: Cornell, 1971), pp. 184–202. Lodge reproduces the original unemended text and discusses a crucial anomaly in the original publication between lines 46 and 69. The problem with the original text is that there is a logical inconsistency between who is saying what to whom. That is, the prolonged direct discourse of the passage makes it difficult to attribute the sentences to a specific character. They in fact overlap. Much could be made of this, and I cannot go into it here, but it seems to me that this argument could be fruitfully followed up in the directions Miller pursues in his interpretations of double reading in *Reading Narrative*.

26 I owe this reference to Beckett to a remarkable paper I heard my friend Arthur Broomfield present at a recent conference in Dublin. I also fondly recollect an engrossing paper I heard the late Wolfgang Iser present at University College Dublin in 2006 on Beckett's *Malone Dies* and *Ping*. In this paper, Iser repeated the word "nothing" over and over until the word became a performative response to Beckett's work, doing again what it said.

27 There is surely also something ludicrously funny about the uncanny. Who has not laughed at the example Freud gives of wandering helplessly into the red-light district of a provincial Italian town three times? See Sigmund Freud, "The Uncanny" (1919) in *The Penguin Freud Library*, 14, trans. James Strachey (London: Penguin, 1985), p. 359.

28 According to Freud's etymological and sociocultural survey of the term, there are all sorts of ambivalent and wonderfully elusive connotations associated with the word "uncanny" (*Unheimlich*). One of which, and the one most often cited in criticisms of this particular work, is Freud's quotation from Schelling: "'Unheimlich' is the name for everything that ought to have remained secret and hidden but has come to light." Sigmund Freud, "The Uncanny" (1919) in *The Penguin Freud Library*, 14, trans. James Strachey (London: Penguin, 1985), p. 345. In his "Repetition and the Uncanny" in *Fiction and Repetition*, Miller makes the point that Emily Brontë's *Wuthering Heights* is uncanny for reasons linked to Freud's notions of repetition, *der Wiederholungszwang*. The emphasis is, therefore, on

the return of the repressed, what comes back, a revenant. Regarding the opening words of the novel, "1801 – I have just returned," Miller says "The reading of the first present-tense words of the novel performs a multiple act of resurrection, an opening of graves or a raising of ghosts. In reading those first words and then the ones that follow to the end, the reader brings back from the grave first the fictive "I" who is supposed to have written them or spoken them . . . With that "I" the reader brings back also the moment in the fall of 1801 when his "I have just returned" is supposed to have been written or spoken. By way of that first "I" and first present moment the reader then resurrects from the dead, with Lockwood's help, in one direction Hindley, Nelly . . . and the rest . . . In the other direction are also evoked first Ellis Bell, the pseudonymous author, who functions as a ghostly name on the title page [then Bell as character and editor]. Ellis Bell is another representative of the reader, overhearing, overseeing, overthinking, and overfeeling what Lockwood says, sees, thinks, feels" etc, p. 71. Like David Copperfield—whose opening words are similarly present-tense performative evocations of the dead, "I am born," or indeed any novel, the act of reading repeats uncannily "a murmuring repetition, something which has been repeating itself incessantly there in the words on the page," p. 72. This act reiterates a linguistic grammatical order which has already been repeated countless times before and will be repeated countless times again in an infinitely recursive series. But in conjuring those ghosts, the reader makes them live again in a new light each time, though each time will be a repetition with a difference.

29   See Charlotte Brontë's *Jane Eyre* (London: Penguin, 2003), p. 19. "The fact is, I was a trifle beside myself; or rather out of myself, as the French would say." I think here also of course of the pseudonymous author and narrator of each work and the perpetual distancing each effects in the process of inscription. From Dickens we move to a fictionalized alter-ego sharing obvious similarities with the author. The narrator is also an author in the novel. So, we move from Charles Dickens to David Copperfield, from CD to DC on the other side of the mirror, so to speak. But what is most interesting about the first-person pseudo-autobiographical novel, as both *Jane Eyre* and *David Copperfield* can be at some levels taken to be, is this awareness that the conscious subject is always already divided within itself, that the "I" is always, as Julia Kristeva would put it, strangers to ourselves—I confirm here that the pronoun agreement in any sentence is always somehow labored, forced, and exclusive. We may also say, as Hillis Miller does in an early essay on *David Copperfield*, that in the autobiographical novel there is always "a moving toward the future in order to come back to what one has already been, in an attempt to complete one's deepest possibility of being

by drawing the circle of time closed and thereby becoming whole. But the circle of time is complete only with my death." In order to know the self as a unified subject, any self, one would have to be dead. In reading a novel, even a novel one has written oneself, the act of reading this I is a raising from the dead in an uncanny process of reliving an-other's subjectivity as a déjà vu, an experience of the double. All readings are raisings of the dead, necromancies, dark arts performed to import knowledge from an unknowable future and an equally unknowable past. See "Three Problems of Fictional Form: First-Person Narration in *David Copperfield* and *Huckleberry Finn*" in *Victorian Subjects*, pp. 97–8.

30 For the best single book on the subject, see Nicholas Royle's *The Uncanny* (Manchester: Manchester University Press, 2003b). Here, echoing what Miller might call Derrida's uncanny criticism, Royle relates in a brilliantly suggestive locution, "Unsettling the ground of both poles (imagination/reality), literature entails the experience of a *suspended* relation," p. 15.

31 For a wonderful paper on Nabokov's allusions to Lewis Carroll's work in *Lolita*, see "Humbert Humbert *Through the Looking Glass*" by Elizabeth Prioleau in *Twentieth Century Literature*, vol. 21, no. 4, 1975, pp. 428–37.

32 For Miller's discussion of virtual automobility, see "Virtual Automobility: Two Ways to Get a Life" in *Against Automobility*, eds. Steffen Böhm, Campbell Jones, Chris Land and Matthew Patterson (Oxford: Blackwell, 2006), pp. 193–207. Here, Miller uses the term "virtual automobility" to describe the process by which "I move outside myself into virtual realities that may make me forget where 'I really am'," p. 193. The "two ways" of the title refers to the difference between a "paper culture" and a "cyberculture," two ways to get another life.

33 For a specific commentary on Miller's reading of this passage, see Julian Wolfreys' *Deconstruction • Derrida* (New York: St. Martin's Press, 1998a), pp. 165–67; Mark Currie's *Postmodern Narrative Theory* (London: Macmillan, 1998), pp. 140–41; and Valentine Cunningham's somewhat exasperated reading of Miller's reading of the yarn in Conrad's *Heart of Darkness* in *Glossalalia: An Alphabet of Critical Keywords* (Edinburgh: Edinburgh University Press, 2003), pp. 353–66: "This keen embroidering of the yarn story with a critical yarn about embroidering seems a mite over-rich, and how a critical yarner can both be in a web and also suspended over a chasm takes a bit of envisaging, and even the blankest of pages are not *chasms*," p. 365. This commentary appears in Cunningham's reading of "Y" as "yarn" in this critical anthology of keywords. The problem with yarning as a figure for narrative is of course that there is no quintessential

ur-yarn, if you will, from which to measure other yarns. There is no figure in the carpet to show how well you've yarned. Once this is glimpsed, the disparity between the kernel and the shell becomes intertwined, sewn into the commentary, perhaps exasperatingly so. But this does nothing to alleviate the sense that Conrad's story is parabolic, disfiguring as it figures, veiling and unveiling without an apocalyptic event of ultimate discovery.

34 The phrase "pardon for not meaning" [*Pardon de ne pas vouloir dire*] comes from Jacques Derrida's wonderfully multivalent essay "Literature in Secret: An Impossible Filiation" in *The Gift of Death*, 2nd edn, trans. David Wills, pp. 119–58. Of this essay, Miller offers the following commentary in *For Derrida*: "Speaking of the enigmatic phrase he uses as a leitmotif in 'Literature in Secret . . . Derrida says: 'And being up in the air is what it keeps its secret of, the secret of a secret which is perhaps not one, and which, because of that fact, announces literature'. If you cannot figure it out, decipher its secret, or even tell for sure whether or not it hides a secret, it must be literature," p. 197.

35 I refer to Derrida's essay "Justices" in *Provocations to Reading* in which Derrida talks of a letter he received from Miller on June 2, 1969: "By the way, my first name is 'Joseph,' not 'John,' not that it matters in the least, since I've never used that name in any case," p. 248. See also Dragan Kujundžić's recent film *The First Sail: J. Hillis Miller* (2012) for Derrida's own commentary on this point. For a great critical introduction to Miller's work on the zero/one question, see also the *Journal for Cultural Research*, vol. 8, no. 2 (April, 2004). This special issue, "Zero and Literature," dedicated to Miller's work on the subject, contains important essays by Derek Attridge, Thomas Docherty, Claudia Egerer, and Roland Munro among others.

AFTERWORD BY
JULIAN WOLFREYS

ABCing you: Raising the stakes
of/for reading or, Miller's Tale

I hesitated long and hard over my title, longer probably than it took to write this essay, on an invitation from Éamonn Dunne, whose wonderful Miller's Tale this is. Bad imitation sub-Joycean puns aside, would the title bear the weight of that ponderous diacritical mark that separates, even as it authorizes the clumsy double copulative, two prepositions joined only be a shared "f." Puns can always be forgiven, at best clever wordplay having a significance beyond the joke, at worst a mere foible, a bagatelle, the signs of an academic too long at the keyboard. But conjoined, jointed, disjointed words? Surely something in academic practice long past its sell-by date, relic of another era, one often not so lovingly referred to, but almost certainly erroneously as "poststructuralism." The point of that disjunction though is very much to the point, and has been introduced to signal what, precisely, is at stake here: a question of good reading, of the kind of good reading on the one hand that has been pursued through various turns by J. Hillis Miller over more than 60 years of publications—and what publications—and, on the other hand, the good reading of those turns, those swerves of reading and writing that Éamonn Dunne has so patiently, so lovingly, pursued in Miller's wake, but also with that fidelity that veers off from mere pursuit, dogged trail following, into

something much more original, much more original, in fact, than
my title, either its play or pun, or what that lays claim to map in my
reading of Dunne reading Miller.

What is traced here though in this exemplary consideration of
Miller unDunne? What is being Dunne in the name of Miller? There
is that alphabetical simplicity for instance. Surely, no good reading
can be claimed for an act that wilfully "reduces" Miller's work in all
its myriad turns over so many years, to the arbitrary sequence, and
structure of the alphabet. What takes place though, if you care to spend
your time considering the stakes of reading, the stakes on the one
hand of reading what the inescapable, irreducible difference between
the stakes *of* reading and the stakes *for* reading as I am suggesting,
somewhat coyly and in passing that you do, in order that you be
faithful both to Miller, to Dunne's Miller; and therefore to Dunne,
what is Dunne in his name, in the name that signifies always already
an act, a commitment, a performative of sorts; then taking that care,
following the tale that takes the shape of an alphabetical reduction,
you will find illuminated for you the care for the word as word.

You will encounter at every link in the alphabetical chain such care
in both Miller and in Dunne reading Miller. You will read an attention
to the reading of the word as word, not as some vehicle or medium to
transport one beyond language all too rapidly, freeing oneself from its
snares, as though one had an aversion to Ariadne's thread, and wanted
only to cut through the skein of language we call the literary in order
to "escape"—escape our responsibilities that reading demands we
take up; here are the stakes *of* reading: what is wagered in the name of
reading, which wager Miller, and Dunne after him pursue; but also,
the stakes *for* reading: what remains to be thought concerning the act

of reading itself, not only as the substrate (from page to screen) from which, by which reading takes place, but also as the very fundamental question of what it means to read the literary, to have the time, to take the time, that is the exorbitant and increasingly unjustifiable luxury that is literary reading, when most academics are concerned more with context than with concept, as though the latter were the dirtiest word in the English language.

To care about such things, to give such attention to the word, and to care to take that care; this is both the hallmark, the countersignature of Miller's work, whether in its earlier, more explicitly phenomenological openings, indebted to, but not simply in imitation of Georges Poulet— already from the Dickens book, there is a departure, a concern with the other of phenomenology, that to which phenomenology cannot turn—or in its later interests in the political stakes of and for reading in general, and why we should concern ourselves *today* and in an unprogrammable future with a nineteenth-century author such as George Eliot, as much as it is a hallmark of Éamonn Dunne's excursive discursive foray into the world and words of Miller's tales of reading.

That there is a reduction of sorts here to alphabetical sequence, structure, and pseudo-order—and it is pseudo-order inasmuch as Dunne, once under way, soon departs from the line he is pursuing, branching off, taking different paths, or simply going off road with Miller—is a recognition that one has to reduce, in some manner not unlike that of a Husserlian reduction, in order to produce an authentic account, the good reading, whether one remains with phenomenology or not—and it has to be said that, in this practice of patient close reading, phenomenology has taught Miller, teaches Dunne in reading Miller, that whether one remains with phenomenology,

phenomenology always remains with one, remaining as the way by which any good reading should move, should engage. While other "readers" might wish things were simpler, clearly, to borrow from Dunne's epigraphs, word has not gotten around that reading is far from simple; while a reduction to the alphabet stakes a claim to a formal approach, it bets, and this is implicitly signaled in its alpha-sequencing, on the very complexity of language taken as language, and that one cannot eschew the demands of reading. Any other act of criticism is simply, and simplistically, the avoidance of responsibility, a guilty act of nonreading hounded by the nightmare of history to which so many critics succumb, but which in their every engagement signals their own complicity in a nightmare they are incapable of reading.

What Dunne does then, what Dunne has dunne, what is being dunne by Dunne is a return to reading, to reading reading as reading reads reading's readings. We read, if we are careful readers, and I quote—so I read—a glimpse of the act of reading in its inventive and surprising acknowledgment of the unique richness of each literary work explored. So, not simply Dunne reading Miller, but Dunne reading Miller reading Proust. If, as Dunne claims, each act of reading is a performative action, a *finding* of what was there already, a local oddness, peculiarity, or anomaly (a favorite word of Miller's, this signaling the very materiality of the text, its singularity and embeddedness within its own cultural and, risk the word, why not, historical moment), then such a performative in liberating what is encrypted is also radically inventive. Here, *invention* signals not the making of the new (idle myth, the very stuff of literary works), but instead, the recognition of what is already there, always already at stake for reading, what stakes its claims as being of significance precisely because it is so seemingly anomalous. Dunne chooses to read closely close readings of Miller's of such anomalous figures, tropes, events within the texts of others, anomalies embedded by virtue of the fact that they have already been *invented*, found at work, found to put significance, and the literary, into play, by the authors whom Miller reads.

So: Dunne reading Miller reading Proust reading the "rhetoricians," who in turn *invent*, who read, read this, read that, read X, Y, or Z, only to find themselves, even as we, in their wake, find ourselves back at the beginning, if we are good readers, much as Joyce insists we need to be when, in the final pages of *Finnegan Wake*, he lets run on a line that takes us back by swerve of shore and bend of bay to the *Wake*'s first page, its illusory "first line" already found, already invented, already underway. Language, Joyce knew, is the wake of history, the word the wake left by the world, in the wake of the world's events; but as Husserl knew, there is only, after experience, after perception of that experience, after re-presentation of that perception of experience through the filters of memory, the trace, the wake. And so there is, there must be the good reader, to follow on, in the wake, to follow the trace, pick up the thread, unraveling in order to understand that which language invents when there is no more experience, when there is no experience as such, save for reading as the experience of the word, in which everything is performed, everything invented. For those of us who believe in the importance of reading, Miller can teach us that we will never be done with it, if we "do" it properly—and there is no right way, only the patient and rigorous reflection on the word, the trace of the other. But what Dunne teaches us about reading, in reading Miller, reading Miller reading, is that we will never be dunne with Miller.

To read is to mill, to put to the grindstone the rougher parts of speech and writing, in order to find the kernel. In order to read then, in order to learn how to read, Dunne reminds us, we need a Miller. That Dunne reads Miller so well is in evidence on every page of the volume you are holding presently and, it is to be hoped, reading. If you are reading it, you will know already that you will never have dunne reading Miller, for Dunne's acts of reading Miller engage us in an endless milling of the possibilities of what language does, what it can do, what it says, what it performs, what it invents. Reading is endless, because if we are always in the wake of reading, in the wake of Dunne in the wake of Miller in the wake of etc., and so on, and so forth, *et ainsi, und so weiter, et cetera* . . . , then we find ourselves engaging not simply with a literary or historical past but in certain ways with a past to come. Though many of Miller's publications appear so eloquently to have the "last word" on a subject, this is not the case. There is no "last word" in good reading, we always have to begin again: begin again Finnegan, in our ending is our beginning, ABCing us on to the limits of our reading but not reading as such. Miller knows there is no last word, and this has been signaled most recently in a book, which, in many ways, is a return, *Reading for Our Time*, in which, in an extravagantly untimely fashion, Miller returns to George Eliot, to *Adam Bede* and *Middlemarch* to be exact, beginning by throwing down the gauntlet, so to speak, for reading, of reading:

> Can reading *Adam Bede* and *Middlemarch* today be at all justified, in this time of irreversible global climate change, worldwide

financial meltdown, with a new financial bubble already building, and the bamboozling of the American electorate (and other electorates around the world) by the media, advertising, the politicians, and hidden right-wing contributors into voting in ways exactly contrary to their interests? What use is "reading for our time"? The Republicans in the last United States general election in November, 2010, took over the House of Representatives and increased their number of conservative Senators. They are determined not just to defeat Obama in the next presidential election, but to real the healthcare reform bill, to privatize or abolish Social Security, to phase out Medicare, to repeal or weaken further the already weak financial regulation bill, to keep tax cuts for the rich, to continue to stalemate any climate legislation, and to carry on indefinitely our war in Afghanistan and our continued presence in Iraq. They have some help in this all from Democrats. If we follow this path, we are throwing ourselves over the cliff. In order to go along with this program of self-destruction, "we the people" have to be persuaded to believe that lies are truths. What possible use can rhetorical readings of *Adam Bede* and *Middlemarch* in these bad times be? Such readings would seem to be a big waste of time. We have far more urgent things to do. In any case, in these days . . . so many people are glued all day to their iPhones and Blackberries . . . Our attention spans . . . reduced to the length of a sound bite or of a 140 character "Tweet."[1]

Yes, yes. And some people would sooner spend their time reading another biography about an author for the details of underwear he allegedly bought his so-called mistress rather than reading his works.

Miller's rhetorical questions frame, and then open onto the culpability our avoidance of reading has led to. Seemingly, having no answer to the question "why read George Eliot," he demonstrates why reading, authentic reading, good reading is now more than ever significant, if we are not all to be "bamboozled" as we go about "well wadded with stupidity" (as a Victorian author has it) and, if not exactly entertaining ourselves to death, then certainly playing with ourselves while Rome, Greece, Spain, Ireland, England, all go into melt down. *Again.*

To the question "why," Miller proposes two answers, "incompatible" with each other: On the one hand, reading is a "good in itself," in a Kantian sense. Simply that. There is a pleasure that does not need justification. On the other hand, though, and with Miller there is always an other hand, the hand of the other coming to take you by the hand, if you're willing to follow in its wake, and be shown what good reading means, what it can do; on the other hand, "some few readers here and there might learn something about how to unmask the lies that bombard us in the real world by reading *Middlemarch* or *Adam Bede* as models for how to do that. . . . Demystifying . . . illusions [lies] for the reader's benefit is the chief goal in the narrators' analysis."[2] To read is to demystify. It is to open oneself to demystification, to run lies, illusions, half truths through the mill of reading in order to sort the wheat from the chaff, rhetorically speaking, but with an eye in speaking rhetorically on what the past may come both to represent and to re-present, in order that reading may open the good reader today, one of the few good readers in any *today* you care to name (and George Eliot, as Miller amply demonstrates, was one, is one such reader, remains one such reader to encounter, to follow in the wake of, to learn from), to a future to come other than that programmed future the media and the politicians would have us sign on for, buy into, a future programmed in the full and cynical knowledge that we are all more interested in the latest winner of *Britain's Got Talent*.

For Miller, the past is always already "represented." Both represented—pictured, constructed, imagined, narrated; Eliot does this better than just about anybody—and re-presented—returned and returning, brought before the eye and the mind, by a mediation of the moment; what we call "past," or "the past," can, in effect or practice, never exist *as such*. "It" is nothing today, save for those traces and marks, events and occasions, which, though singular, maintain an iterable communication between the time of inscription and the times of reception, reading, translation, interpretation, and invention. To this extent—and this is already a great deal—what is called "the past," though no longer an existent present as such, and being "nothing" save for its echoes, transmissions, remnants, and ruins, remains as memory work, as that which comes to return, always becoming. In this, in being "spectral," it is re-membered, and so remains as that which, though appearing to return from a past historical site also, always, remains to come. The past is not a future, not something certain. It is, instead, a past *to-come*; it is, to borrow a distinction made by Jacques Derrida apropos the different modalities of futurity, *l'avenir* rather than *le future*. The "past" is to be remembered, narrated, accounted for, faced up and responded to, borne witness to, and *made to appear* from what is always already left; though it is also that which is, equally, imminent, invisible, the other side of a threshold the limit of which is what is there as opposed to what is not there but which, nevertheless makes itself felt or otherwise perceived, more or less indirectly. And this making-appear of that which is to come is, if a work of memory, also one of invention, the invention of reading, that is reading, where one finds rather than creates what has been left, what remains mute, and so give the silenced trace a voice, a new inscription, a new re-presentation.

To engage with such a reading though means getting back to basics, returning to, or allowing to return, to re-present themselves, our ABCs. Miller reading: Proust, Eliot, de Man, Derrida. In every example, this is what we might learn, if we aspire at all to being one of the few good readers. And this is what Éamonn Dunne seeks to show us, this is what he has dunne, in reading with care, insight, and responsibility, the ABCs of Miller's tale.

Notes

1   J. Hillis Miller, *Reading for our Time:* Adam Bede *and* Middlemarch *Revisited* (Edinburgh: Edinburgh University Press, 2012), xi.

2   Ibid., xii.

ANNOTATED BIBLIOGRAPHY OF MAJOR WORKS BY J. HILLIS MILLER

Charles Dickens: The World of his Novels

CAMBRIDGE, MA: 1958

A classic work in Dickens criticism and still being used on many undergraduate college courses today, the volume is a model of penetrating, sympathetic, and concise critical analyses of the complete Dickens novels in chronological order. Dedicated to Georges Poulet, a major figure in "phenomenological criticism," the book explores the unique pulse of Dickens' imaginative landscape, the "interior space" or "life-world" of his writings, and posits a criticism of consciousness whereby Dickens' literary journey is one of continuing self-recognition. Its strength as a general introduction to the works of Dickens is obvious, as is its debt to a certain radiance of Pouletian criticism, though its real strength is assuredly Miller's focus on the *style* of the works themselves, the remarkable close readings of central moments in *Pickwick Papers, Oliver Twist, Marin Chuzzlewit, Bleak House, Great Expectations*, and *Our Mutual Friend* that distinguishes the book from its theoretical underpinnings.

[A digitized version of this book is now available online with a new Preface by the author: http://victorian.lang.nagoya-u.ac.jp/dickens/miller-dickens.pdf] accessed 3/13/2013.

The Disappearance of God: Five Nineteenth-Century Writers (Cambridge, MA: Harvard University Press, 1963).

With chapters on Thomas De Quincey, Robert Browning, Emily Brontë, Matthew Arnold and Gerard Manley Hopkins, this volume concentrates on each writer's entire corpus individually and from the perspective of a unique monadological mind struggling to come to terms with a universe where the image of God is neither immanent (the romantics) nor dead (Nietzsche's "Gott ist tot") but transcendent. If the Dickens book is notable for its concise explication of all Dickens' novels between two covers, then *The Disappearance of God* is exemplary for condensing the entire works (essays, poems, plays, novels, notebooks etc) of each of its five writers between chapter headings. The strategy here is to identify a profound sense of loss or longing in each writer as a touchstone for a spiritual "point of departure" that defines and redefines that personality, or to use Hopkins's peculiar neologisms, the "selftaste" or "inscape" of that writer. The dizzying condensation and distillation, what Miller refers to as the "systole and diastole of criticism," culminates in a richly textured work that often finds the reader vacillating rapidly between extravagant panoramic prospects and delicate interpretations of minutely rendered details. The tendency is to feel that after each chapter one has been privy to the entire works of the writer under discussion. Miller has also written three separate prefaces for this book, each testifying anew to the work's enduring fascination for him.

Poets of Reality: Six Twentieth-Century Writers (Cambridge, MA: Harvard University Press, 1965).

A companion book to *The Disappearance of God*, *Poets of Reality* extrapolates the ontological question in the wake of God through readings of Joseph Conrad, W. B. Yeats, T. S. Eliot, Dylan Thomas, Wallace Stevens, and William Carlos Williams. Whereas a nineteenth-century Zeitgeist articulated the transcendence of God, a God at an unattainable remove from society, symbolism, and art, here the twentieth-century experiences the death of God, a God that no longer exists. This theothanatological model is pervasive in twentieth-century literature and each writer in this volume, in his own singular aspect, attempts to reconnect with the absolute reality of being in a world without divine sanction. Yet again Miller's peculiar prowess as a scrupulous close reader is exemplified throughout, though most powerfully in the superb last two chapters on Wallace Stevens and William Carlos Williams.

The Form of Victorian Fiction (Notre Dame: University of Notre Dame, 1968).

Undoubtedly a much neglected work, it is made up of four short chapters presented as the Ward-Philips Lectures at the University of Notre Dame in 1967. The book's brevity is certainly at odds with the promises of its chapter titles and might seem somewhat off-putting to a novice reader as a result. This is certainly justifiable as "Time and Intersubjectivity," "The Ontological Basis of Form," "The Narrator as General Consciousness," and "Self and Community" are weighty issues deserving a much fuller commentary than the space provided here. They are in truth issues that will haunt much of Miller's subsequent writing, which is why this slim volume is so fascinating as a touchstone for Miller studies in general. Much of this fascination arises from the tension between, on the one hand, existential and historical arguments (a hangover from the earlier spiritual histories) and, on the other hand, intensifying rhetorical, linguistic interests. Anyone seriously interested in indirect discourse and irony (see also *Reading Narrative* below), community and intersubjectivity, rhythms and temporalities in Victorian literature, fictions of realism, and performative language should consult readings of Eliot's *Middlemarch*, Thackeray's *Henry Esmond*, Dickens' *Our Mutual Friend*, and Trollope's *Ayala's Angel* here.

Thomas Hardy: Distance and Desire (Cambridge, MA: Harvard University Press, 1970).

Another book concentrating wholly on the writing of one author, *Thomas Hardy: Distance and Desire* follows familiar strategic lines by mixing commentary on novels, poems, private notebooks, the verse-play *The Dynasts*, short stories, and Florence Hardy's biography simultaneously, so that poems and notes from the later period can intermingle with and highlight recurring themes and patterns in the novels. In avoiding the chronological novel-by-novel approach, Miller weaves a densely patterned tapestry of Hardy's entire corpus around several important motifs concerning distance and desire: the "distance" is that experience in oneself that creates a longing for the love of another in order to fulfill an "emotional void" and the "desire" is that which propels Hardy's alienated characters out into the world striving toward their inevitable tragic fates, since that love can never be fully realized. Mapping the idiosyncratic universe of Hardy's entire corpus across the various manifestations of characters having fallen in and out of love, we find here a voyeuristic Hardy spying at varying distances on his wonderfully wrought artistic creations. Deft, interpenetrating readings of Hardy' personal relationships, his narrators' relationships with the characters in his stories, and those characters' social bonds are combined and controlled with élan and provide readers of this book with an exceedingly uncommon view of Hardy's exquisite texts.

Fiction and Repetition: Seven English Novels (Cambridge, MA: Harvard University Press, 1982).

Appearing a full twelve years since his last book, *Fiction and Repetition* marks a watershed movement from historical fictions to close textual analyses; in this case of Conrad's *Lord Jim*, Brontë's *Wuthering Heights*, Thackeray's *Henry Esmond*, Hardy's *Tess of the d'Ubervilles* and *The Well-Beloved*, and Woolf's *Mrs. Dalloway* and *Between the Acts*. Asking how methodological presuppositions can guide critics to valid interpretations of particular novels, the book hypothesizes two ways of viewing repetitions in literature that might help us glimpse the peculiar manner in which literary texts have a strange way of exceeding theoretical frameworks. Platonic repetition classically figures a repetition of an archetypal form—an ideal, fixed image, Plato's bed, for instance, is the progenitor of all subsequent imitations. The second form is Nietzschean: all repetition is repetition with a difference, the archetype is an illusion. Though both forms seem mutually exclusive, they are in fact tied up with each other (in a logic of noncontradiction) and, by varying degrees, present themselves in each of the texts Miller chooses. Miller's hypersensitive reading of recurring motifs, memory, and fate in *Tess* is a highlight, as is the uncanny in *Wuthering Heights* and pervasive ironies in Thackeray's *Henry Esmond*. Though the debt to Derrida's thinking is evident throughout the book, a central argument is that theory and reading are also asymmetrical, so that what is of value here are the attempts to account for what happens when he reads those seven novels. The reader is left to his or her own judgments on the issue, but the incisiveness of the interpretations, their generosity and erudition, is often stunningly original, making this work a good starting point for readers who are new to Miller's writings.

The Linguistic Moment: From Wordsworth to Stevens (Princeton: Princeton University Press, 1985).

As its title suggests, the book is concerned with those moments in literature when the language itself becomes foregrounded and problematic. Examining eight poets—Wordsworth, Shelley, Browning, Hopkins, Hardy, Yeats, Williams, and Stevens—Miller traces the moments in their works when thematic and narrative elements subside in lieu of a hypnotic vacillation between figurative and literal language. The master trope of this interplay is *catachresis*, a suspended word, which is neither simply literal nor figurative but a placeholder for the inexpressible. Catachresis names, by way of an abusive substitution or displacement, that which has no proper name, for example, the "leg" of a chair or the "eye" of a storm. Miller's essay on Stevens' "The Rock" is a master class in the linguistic momentum of catachresis as it moves from grounding to ungrounding critical commentary on the poem. His chapter on Yeats' "Nineteen Hundred and Nineteen" provides another extraordinary example of a poem that puts its own medium in question by helplessly circling what Miller calls an "unknown X beyond language." The book is heavily indebted to Nietzsche's work on metaphor and also to Derrida's, though its real importance leads out from those moments of reading that seems so often to challenge and suspend the theoretical import. The "Preface" and "Postface" to the book are symptomatic of this tension: "Between Theory and Practice" and "Between Practice and Theory," respectively.

The Ethics of Reading: Kant, de Man, Eliot, Trollope, James, and Benjamin (New York: Columbia University Press, 1987).

Usually, the first book that springs to mind when people discuss Miller's work, *The Ethics of Reading* marks a decisive point in Miller's career and a work that polarizes many critics even today. Indeed, both this work and the one that follows, *Versions of Pygmalion*, have collectively garnered the most criticism of any of Miller's other works. Consisting of six brief chapters, *The Ethics of Reading* challenges assumptions that rhetorical critics like Miller or de Man are nihilistic or given to value the indeterminacy of all texts in such a way that they can say whatever they like about them. On the contrary, says Miller, there is in any reading an ineluctable obligation, an ethical response and responsibility. The question becomes to whom or to what am I responsible in reading? The approach is, therefore, to examine six authors at specific moments when they reflect on their own acts of reading, which Miller in turn takes as paradigmatic for ethical approaches to the question of reading, teaching, and talking about literature in general. The hypothesis is that without storytelling there is no theory of ethics, so that studying stories is in some way innately connected with what Henry James calls the conduct of life. Miller's readings of Kant, de Man, Eliot, Trollope, James, and Benjamin are all self-consciously performative not simply constative; they are acts of re-reading, so that it is easy to see how Miller's own readings are also part of what he calls an ethics of reading. An extraordinary example of the latter is Miller's reading of "ethicity" in a passage from de Man's *Allegories of Reading* and a subsequent chapter on George Eliot's famous discourse on realism in Chapter 17 of *Adam Bede*. Readers coming to Miller for the first time will find this volume challenging, especially perhaps the chapter on Kant, but slow reading of this book is rewarding, provocative and, particularly, instructive in how attention to detail is paramount for Miller.

Versions of Pygmalion (Cambridge, MA: Harvard University Press, 1990).

Astonishing in its rigorous rhetorical examination of several key works by Henry James, Heinrich von Kleist, Herman Melville, Maurice Blanchot and, of course, Ovid's *Metamorphosis*, *Versions of Pygmalion* completes the theoretical investigations inaugurated in *The Ethics of Fiction*. The latter work ends with a promise to account for an ethics of fiction through sustained investigations into literary works rather than to provide passages where authors are simply reflecting on their works. That promise ensures that this work is not only an explication or unfolding of some theoretical impetus but a performative new start that shows how rhetorical reading is fundamentally tied to local and personal as well as broader political, social, and institutional issues. At the heart of what Miller says of an ethics of reading is the belief that there is no ethics without stories and no stories without prosopopoeias (personifications), that there is an intrinsic and peculiar relationship between stories and ethics. Indeed, it would be better to say that reading places unseen obligations on us. Those obligations are explored here through Miller's own responses to several literary works. The claim is that each reading is a putting into question of the theoretical apparatuses that Miller himself has brought with him to those texts. Understanding good reading in Miller's sense here is to understand that each reading is in its own way inaugural, disruptive, and unforeseeable. Reading in this way causes us to understand that there is no single theory capable of predicting what will happen when a given text is read at a given time; indeed a responsible response means putting any theoretical proclivity in doubt. Miller's readings of Kleist's "Der Findling," Melville's "Bartelby the Scrivener," and James' *What Maisie Knew* are not merely highlights of this volume; they are also examples of Miller at the pinnacle of his powers as a reader.

Tropes, Parables, Performatives: Essays on Twentieth-Century Literature (Harvester Wheatsheaf, 1990); *Victorian Subjects* (Durham: Duke University Press, 1991); *Theory Now and Then* (Durham: Duke University Press, 1991).

Taken together, these three books (appearing at roughly the same time) are testament to Miller's astonishing productivity as an essayist. Comprising sixty-one essays in total, ranging from the King James Bible to "The Function of Literary Theory in the Present Time" (1989), these titles represent almost forty years of publication. The range, of course, is astounding. In *Theory Now and Then*, we encounter essays on the phenomenological criticisms of the Geneva School and Georges Poulet—significant for Miller's first four books—essays on deconstruction and pedagogy, possibly Miller's most famous single essay, "The Critic as Host," as well as essays on de Man, Nietzsche, Stevens, and the presidential address for the 1986 MLA conference, "The Triumph of Theory, the Resistance to Reading, and the Question of the Material Base." *Tropes, Parables, Performatives* focuses on twentieth-century works, beginning with an essay on D. H. Lawrence from 1952. This is followed by essays on Kafka, Woolf, Conrad, and several on Williams, Hardy, and Stevens respectively. *Victorian Subjects* covers, accordingly, the Victorian era and represents Hopkins, Trollope, Eliot, and Carlyle, but especially essays on Dickens. The preface to each of these works eschews a coherent formulation and concentrates on the act of each reading as a singular, unpredictable, anomalous event. In the preface to the latter work, for instance, Miller claims that the title pertains, in one of its variations, to the way each work subjects the reader to some unprecedented otherness, something transformative, evasive, and variable. That said, these works are also powerful reflections of the changing landscapes of theory and criticism since the early fifties. They are also, undoubtedly, a catalog of some of Miller's most exemplary readings and evidence of the powerful aura of all those "others" that compel him to write in the manner that he does.

Hawthorne and History: Defacing It (Cambridge, MA: Basil Blackwell, 1991).

Hawthorne and History is one of a series of books entitled *The Bucknell Lectures in Literary Theory* edited by Michael Payne and Harold Schweizer. Other volumes in the series include important lectures on theory by Barbara Johnson, Frank Kermode, and Stanley Cavell. The real beauty of the series is the manner in which it combines an invited lecture with an informed introduction to each scholar's work, an interview, and a comprehensive bibliography. Though the latter has since been displaced by Julian Wolfreys' comprehensive bibliography in *The J. Hillis Miller Reader* and various online resources, the introduction to this volume and the interview with Martin Heusser and Harold Schweizer are superb for readers interested in getting a good overall introduction to Miller. Indeed, the judicious introduction begins with Miller's 1952 PhD dissertation, "Dickens' Symbolic Imagery," and ends with *The Ethics of Reading* and a prelude to Miller's reading of Nathaniel Hawthorne's short story "The Minister's Black Veil" (1836) which follows. Miller's argument here is woven through Hawthorne's dark allegorical tale of Reverend Hooper, who turns up for his Sunday sermon wearing a black semitransparent veil. The congregation and townspeople naturally begin to wonder what the reason is for this strange compulsion, but Hawthorne never divulges the secret, if there is one. The story, Miller claims, is a kind of double bind in which the reader is caught in a crime the story itself condemns. Hawthorne's story questions the impossibility of not projecting a name or a face or a voice on an inanimate series of marks. In doing so, it dramatizes the act of reading, not just of the minister's veil but also of all those marks on the page that give voice to an absent personality or a human face. The violence of unveiling is a crime the story condemns and puts into play by showing us that prosopopoeia, the fundamental trope of narrative, is inevitable no matter how we theorize it. By the time we come to see that we are committing the crime the story condemns it is too late. We have already projected a face and developed a rationale for Hopper and Hawthorne. History, Miller concludes in the final pages, is analogous to an ideological double bind occurring in Hawthorne's tale, the fundamental linguistic error of projecting a name or a face on the inanimate or the dead.

Ariadne's Thread: Story Lines (New Haven: Yale University Press, 1992).

Ariadne's Thread arose, says Miller, from a failed preface to *Fiction and Repetition* (1982). The plan had been to write a 20-page introduction to the concept of repetition in narrative theory. After 100 pages of manuscript had been written, Miller realized he was writing another book, hence the present work and the four other books that make up the Ariadne's thread project. Comprised of only four chapters, two long and two short, Miller traces four topics in narrative theory: line, character, anastomosis (image of a line joining two vessels), and figure. To trace the labyrinth, as Miller is conscious throughout this book, is to recreate it, and the book's overriding virtue is to place reading at the heart of that labyrinth. Indeed, Miller's reading of Goethe's *Die Wahlverwandtschaften* (*Elective Affinities*) in the long chapter on anastomosis (interpersonal relations) is beautifully rendered and sensitive to Goethe's own presupposition that reading is the originating and central moment of subjective life. To exist, Miller gleans from Goethe's novel, is to read and to be read. Dramatizing both an ontological reading and a rhetorical reading at once, Goethe's novel then enacts an impasse that the critic cannot surmount because each way of reading undoes its counterpart. No road will lead to the center of the labyrinth of narrative theory, Miller also suggests, since the relation of language in narrative is not between sign and thing but between sign and sign in a system of differences that draws its meaning from other signs. The language of narrative theory is, therefore, catachresis through and through, a sign for sign relationship in a series that begins with a narrative line and forms a möbius loop for criticism. No vantage point, Miller argues, exists outside of reading to explain what happens there. We can only follow thread after thread to see why this is the case; we can only follow all those story lines to see for ourselves how it happens and where it leads.

Illustration (Cambridge, MA: Harvard University Press, 1992).

A significant contribution to debates in cultural studies, *Illustration* aims to map out some subtle and significant differences between rhetorical criticism and a broader cultural criticism emerging in the early 1990s. Through its own illustrations, verbal, graphic, thematic, and political, *Illustration* illustrates the impossibility of harmoniously combining linguistic with pictorial representation. In doing this, it sets out by describing seven presuppositions persisting in cultural studies before examining the ways in which digitization was beginning to effect reading and theory at the time. Indeed, Miller argues that the layout of this book itself imagines a hypertext version whereby the reader would be able to click on various sections and be taken down disparate and unforeseeable pathways. In offering close interpretations of various art works—from Phiz's illustrations of Dickens' novels and placemats from a hotel in Virginia to J. M. W. Turner and Vincent van Gough's celebrated paintings—Miller focuses on the importance of close rhetorical reading and the inaugural power of each artwork to bring something new into the world. The result is a series of powerfully suggestive readings, a compelling defense of the cultural significance of art, and an argument for vigilant rhetorical re-examinations in cultural studies at large.

Topographies (Stanford: Stanford University Press, 1995).

The word "topography" combines the Greek word *topos*, meaning place, with the Greek word *graphein*, to write. Teasing out the myriad implications, slippages, and translations of this word, Miller investigates ways in which topographical metaphors act in philosophical and literary discourses to both orientate and disorient the reader. Offering rigorous readings of works by Kleist, Hardy, Heidegger, Derrida, Dickens, the Book of Ruth, Nietzsche, Faulkner, and so on, Miller asks of each text how it generates an imaginative landscape and how it gives meaning to that placeless place. There are many highlights in this book that make it a personal favorite, including extraordinary readings of law in Heinrich von Kleist's story "Michael Kohlhaas;" promises in Dickens' *Pickwick Papers*; Wallace Stevens' "The Idea of Order at Key West;" and Jacques Derrida's topographies. Though each chapter pays particular attention to the creation of place in theory and fiction, the book is also notable for its thinking on ethics, justice, responsibility, and translation. For anyone interested in watching Dragan Kujundžić's film on J. Hillis Miller, *The First Sail*, Chapter 5 "Temporal Topographies: Tennyson's Tears" is a must read, since Miller says in *The First Sail* that it was his initial reaction to this poem that made him decide to pursue literary study as a vocation.

Reading Narrative (Norman: University of Oklahoma Press, 1998).

Reading Narrative closes out the so-called Ariadne's Thread project which Miller began working on in his notebooks in 1976. *Fiction and Repetition* (1982), *Ariadne's Thread* (1992), *Illustration* (1992), and *Topographies* have all sprung, says Miller in the preface to *Reading*

Narrative, from his obsession with line imagery in narratives. As a culmination of that project, this is a stunning example of what Miller terms, in an illuminating neologism, "ananarratology" (discussed in "b" above). Arguing against structuralist narratological claims that a science of narrative is possible, this book repeatedly and impressively shows how story lines are always (already) explicitly or implicitly redoubling, wander off course, derailing, distilling, or otherwise complicating logocentric assumptions concerning beginnings, middles, and ends. These arguments are investigated through rigorous readings of Sophocles' *Oedipus the King* (and Aristotle's commentaries on that in *Poetics*) in the book's powerful and convincing opening chapter. Subsequent chapters also investigate line imagery through ends, beginnings, middles (in that order), figures, multiplications, dialogics, anacoluthons, and arabesques. The book is, therefore, both rigorous and intensely playful in its attention to the winding and unwinding labyrinthine paths of narrative discourse. Quite apart from the influential reading of Shakespeare's *Troilus and Cressida*, "Ariachne's Broken Woof," and Miller's impressive interpretations of works by Henry James, Laurence Sterne, Proust, Balzac, and Elizabeth Gaskell, the book's highlight for this reader is the impressive chapter on indirect discourse and irony. Miller has had quite a lot to say about the latter elsewhere in his work, though I recommend this chapter as one of the best starting points into thinking through Miller's continued fascination with irony in both literature and theory.

Black Holes (Stanford: Stanford University Press, 1999).

Set alongside Manuel Asensi's *Boustrophedonic Reading* so that that two books face each other on alternate pages in a single volume, *Black*

Holes is haunted by a commentary that faces it from an opposite page. To say that Miller himself has also been haunted by something other is a good starting point for approaching this text. Time and again throughout his career Miller has claimed that the local strangeness of anomalous speech acts in literary works has driven him to become the critic he is. Another term for that pervasive oddness that Miller claims can't be fully grasped in reading would be black holes. Miller dedicates this book to the memory of Bill Readings and the book is heavily indebted to the arguments Readings sets forth in his seminal work *The University in Ruins*. The opening chapter, for example, explores the crisis in the university's idea of itself and the questions arising from the practical use of humanities in a time of globalization and technologization. Miller's conception of a university of dissensus is compelling and leads to some fascinating arguments, as is his readings of fractal images in Proust and the concluding chapter on the excess of reading and the university to come. From a personal perspective, the highlight of the book is the discussion of the grounds of love in Anthony Trollope's *Ayala's Angel*, where Ayala's declarations of love spiral into encounters with otherness and black holes in the literary universe.

Speech Acts in Literature (Stanford: Stanford University Press, 2001).

As its title suggests (see my preface), *Speech Acts in Literature* is an attempt to explain the importance of speech act theory for literary study. The book arose, Miller claims, out of an attempt to write a brief introduction to speech acts for another book he was writing on Henry James. Taking a discussion of J. L. Austin's magnum opus, *How to Do Things with Words*, as its opening chapter, Miller proceeds to discuss

Jacques Derrida's devastating critique of John Searle's criticism in *Limited Inc*, Paul de Man's attention to irony in speech acts, Wittgenstein's attention to emotions in speech acts, as well as Proust's others. In this work, Miller is often devastatingly funny. Picking up on the cool irony of Austin's *How to Do Things with Words*, Miller has a lot of fun punning and joking on the peculiarities of Austin's hilarious examples. I know of no other criticism of Derrida's *Limited Inc* that is so clear and inviting. Readers of this book will almost certainly find themselves approaching Derrida's *Limited Inc* with a renewed fervor. They will also realize the importance of studying speech act theory for advancement in literary studies.

Others (Princeton: Princeton University Press, 2001).

Not *the* other but others. Much theoretical discussion over the years has focused on notions of the other as a concept of racial, ethnic, or gendered otherness. The other has been conceived of as something alien, inferior, or exotic, something odd, queer, foreign. Here, Miller claims that he has always been haunted by a "sense" of radical otherness in literary works, a "sense" that some intense otherness is mediated through the verbal features of the texts he reads in the always unique event of reading them. Though the book begins and ends with theorists, Miller also claims that no abstract theorizing or conceptualization can get you to a sense of this otherness. Only acts of reading, performative acts, acts which inaugurate by bringing something new into the sphere of understanding, can bring you close to the nonconcept of what Jacques Derrida has otherwise called *le tout autre*. Speaking of the other in the singular form is a way of domesticating or personifying a radical otherness that Miller wishes to put in play throughout this work, so he asks that readers resist the temptation to think of a unified or single entity. The result is 11 chapters of remarkably close and sensitive readings, readings of compelling intimacy and verve. Each essay extends the notion of otherness by seeing it as pervasive, not different but intrinsic, inherent, symptomatic. Highlights include the opening chapter on irony and myth in Friedrich Schlegel, a stunning reading of Yeats' "The Cold Heaven" and the penultimate chapter on Paul de Man as allergen. The book opens and closes with this quotation from Jacques Derrida: "the other calls [something] to come and that does not happen except in multiple voices."

On Literature (New York: Routledge, 2002).

Undoubtedly the best starting point for anyone coming to Miller for the first time, *On Literature* is nothing short of a passionate defense of literature's continuing influence on our lives, and a wonderful exemplification of the intense pleasure Miller himself derives from reading literary works. The book might be described as a miniscule "open sesame" into the workings of Miller's own particular concerns with reading literature and theory. One of the recurring motifs in Miller's corpus is an uncompromising attention to the inimical strangeness of literature, for that which cannot be accounted for in literary works. One term for this is literature's "otherness," another term would be its "singularity." What has been most impressive in Miller's books and essays over the years is the exemplary manner in which these complexities are opened up, the way in which this strangeness is brought to the surface. A central argument in the book is what Miller calls the "aporia of reading." In order to enter into the peculiar virtual reality of literature, we must read in some sense innocently, by which is meant a suspension of the critical faculties— what Coleridge famously called the "suspension of disbelief." On the other hand, Miller advocates "good reading": slow, close, critical attention to detail. The latter is a further suspension of the former still, so that the two may actually be incompatible, impossible. In turning through this impossible dilemma—in Miller's terms reading *lento* (slowly) and *allegro* (quickly) at once—there is often a poignant and naive nostalgia for the powers of literature to enthrall us as it did when we read as children and simultaneously a clear-eyed awareness that in our hypermediated, critical age that nostalgia may indeed be lost forever. Of course, one can't be too quick to condemn the critical faculty and Miller doesn't do this either. My advice, however, is to read *The Swiss Family Robinson* before you read this book and then to relinquish yourself (however impossibly) to an extraordinarily touching and insightful work.

Zero Plus One (València: Universitat de València, 2003).

How do you get from zero to one? Or from zero to zero plus one? A short book published by *Biblioteca Javier Coy d'estudis nord-americans* under the auspices of the Universitat de València, *Zero Plus One* consists of two essays: one on zero and the other on the crisis in comparative literature. Miller recounts in the preface to this slim 100-page volume that the space between zero and one figures an infinite abyss. Once you start thinking about it, the argument goes, it becomes unfathomable. Thinking for instance of the origins of zero, Miller traces the figure through semantics, mathematics, physics, philosophy, theology, rhetoric, and economics. And this all occurs in a few brief and playfully ironic introductory pages. This is then followed by the readings of Wolfgang Iser, Maurice Blanchot, and Paul de Man on zero in literature. Much of the fun in this book arises from the obvious enjoyment Miller himself derives in teasing out all sorts of implications for zero—including catachresis, otherness, *khora*, and the fact that zero both is and is not a number, "the nothing that is not there and the nothing that is" according to Wallace Stevens. By turns ludic and rigorous, Miller's story of O is at once fascinating and eloquent, but it is difficult get hold of in more ways than one.

Literature as Conduct: Speech Acts in Henry James (New York: Fordham University Press, 2005).

The word "conduct" in Miller's title has various resonances. Used as a verb, it can mean, simply, to carry something from one place to another; as a noun, it can describe also the way one behaves or acquits oneself. Putting things in words, according to Henry James in his preface to *The Golden Bowl*, is a way of doing something that does other things in turn. Inscribing words on a page, for example, is one way of doing things with words, creating speech that acts, in the strong sense of that word. James calls this, via Ralph Waldo Emerson, the conduct of life. In this work, Miller explores James' work through speech act theory and unravels intricate layers of James' fiction, wherein characters promise, lie, declare love for one another, testify, and so on. All of these speech acts *do* something, just as the reader is *doing* something when he puts those words into commentary, criticism, or teaching. Miller's claim in this work is that understanding how words act performatively, though one can never fully measure the result of a given speech act, is an indispensible tool for understanding literary works. In six chapters, Miller covers topics relating to responsibilities in reading, decisions, community, perjury, and personification. The short opening chapter on "The Aspern Papers" is a brilliant analysis of the act of reading as violation, while subsequent chapters on *The Portrait of a Lady* and *The Wings of the Dove* combine lucid analyses of Derrida, de Man, and Austin with brilliant interrogations of what it means to be in love, to kiss, to decide, to promise, to testify, and to enter into the virtual space of a literary work. Readers interested in seeing how questions raised in speech act theory can provoke magisterial readings of literary texts should start here.

For Derrida (New York: Fordham University Press, 2009).

For Derrida is less a book, in the traditional sense of that term, than a collection of essays responding to disparate or heterogeneous elements in Derrida's writings. Each chapter is a meticulous response to a single word or theme that inevitably spirals out into discussions of the larger Derridean corpus, but the impetus is assuredly directed to a few key moments in those works: decision, *destinerrance*, telepathy, community, performativity, family, responsibility, autoimmunity, and so on. The strength of the volume is its care for Derrida, its moving, personal account of over 40 years of unclouded friendship, its incomplete mourning, and its sensitive responsiveness to the minutiae of the texts it reads—what Miller refers to as "micrological reading"—as well as its cautiousness and consistent appeal to readers to read Derrida's original works. *For Derrida* argues, however paradoxically, that the only way to talk sensibly about Derrida is to avoid generalizing about these key terms, to dispense with the hearsay and the cant, and to go back to the texts themselves, something Miller has been doing consistently since 1965 in the original French. With this in mind, that "*For*" in Miller's title ought to concern its readers a little more than it might do. The book is for Derrida, a gift to his memory; it is for him because it ventriloquizes him. But that "*For*" harbors, to this reader's ear, the performative force of a golfer's exclamation to watch your head, since what you find there might not be all that good for you to know. Chapter 10, "Derrida's Politics of Autoimmunity," is a case in point.

The Medium is the Maker: Browning, Freud, Derrida and the New Telepathic Ecotechnologies (Brighton and Portland: Sussex Academic Press, 2009).

Certainly Miller's funniest work to date, *The Medium is the Maker* argues against Marshall McLuhan's famous dictum (the medium is the message) by claiming that the word *poeisis* means making—poetry, literature makes. The medium is not a passive conduit of meaning, but a performative force that has power to make something happen. Miller's miming of Derrida, Browning, and Freud in this work is also a form of happening, self-consciously so, since in this work Miller becomes a medium for each of his three interlocutors. He raises them from the dead, remakes them in his own inimitable fashion, voices their opinions, and draws out the irony at large in their works. Apart from some sombre moments of reminiscence and anecdote, this gives rise to wonderfully playful speculations regarding his reading of Freud's essays on telepathy, and furthermore of Derrida's readings of those essays and his readings of those yet again. A slim volume, at less than a 100 pages, *The Medium* is remarkable for its hilarious reading of Robert Browning's scatological poem, "Mr. Sludge, c'est moi," its critique of Freud's "fake" lectures on telepathy (designed to put their audience to sleep!), and most particularly, its penetrating commentaries on Derrida's own "wild" essay "Telepathy." Here, Miller claims that deconstruction is a form of comic miming, a way of drawing out ironic undertones by repeating what has already been said by others—like an insolent student repeating his teacher's lesson. Readers will find that Miller can do this with aplomb.

The Conflagration of Community: Fiction Before and After Auschwitz (Chicago: University of Chicago Press, 2011).

Sensitively challenging Theodor Adorno's much-cited maxim that to write a single poem after Auschwitz is barbaric and Elie Wiesel's claims that a novel with Auschwitz as its subject is not a novel, the book explores how literary works can bear testimony to catastrophic and inhuman events such as the Holocaust and the history of slavery in the United States. The first of the book's four parts compares Jean-Luc Nancy's *The Inoperative Community* (from which Miller takes his title) with Wallace Stevens' depiction of an ideal indigenous community in his poem "The Auroras of Autumn." Part 2 collects three chapters on Franz Kafka's novels, reflecting on the prophetic nature of those works and how they perversely foreshadow Auschwitz and the Holocaust, whereas parts 3 and 4 trace testimonies in literature produced by survivors and nonsurvivors after Auschwitz. These are Thomas Keneally's *Schindler's List*, Ian McEwan's *Black Dogs*, Art Spiegelman's *Maus*, and Imre Kertész's *Fatelessness*. The final part is a reading of Toni Morrison's stunning novel *Beloved* in terms of Morrison's peculiar neologism, "rememory," as an implacable demand not only not to forget but also to realize that reading this work can be a productive way of noticing civil rights abuses in the world today. The book's crowning achievement though is Miller's reading of Kertész's *Fatelessness*, where he claims the closer novels get to direct representation of the Shoah, the more rhetorically sophisticated they become and the less likely they are to want to affirm community. The result is a careful reading of the exuberant linguistic and narratological strategies employed by Kertész in an attempt to account for what is in actuality unaccountable. Though Miller claims the book is not a memoir, it is certainly his most personal book to date and a profound testimony in its own right, through the literatures of testimony, both historical and autobiographical, to the appalling genocides perpetrated in a so-called civilized Western world.

The First Sail: J. Hillis Miller (dir.) Dragan Kujundžić (Deer Isle Productions, 2011): Running time: 85 mins.

The First Sail is the first film devoted exclusively to the work and life of J. Hillis Miller. In an interview elsewhere, the director, Dragan Kujundžić, describes the film as belonging to the genre of "fan cinema," and it is easy to see that the motivation behind the project is his deep personal connection with J. Hillis Miller and a real passion for his work. Edited from over 30 hours of footage, *The First Sail* movingly winds through interviews, anecdotes, family histories, lectures, and of course images of Miller sailing boats, which is an abiding fascination for him and a central motif of the film. The film's real benefit for audiences unfamiliar with Miller derives from those filmed lectures and intimate discussions. In one touching moment, Miller is seen watching a recording of Jacques Derrida presenting a lecture on his work. Miller claims that he is moved by this, "but not to tears," since he is aware of the denaturing effect of the medium. Watching Derrida, Miller speaks of the command Derrida had over his audiences; the turns of phrase, the punning on multiple languages, the smiles and gestures that made Derrida a master performer. Much the same can be said of Miller's lectures and Kujundžić brings this across beautifully. Miller is nothing if not entertaining and instructive on all sorts of subjects, including literature, philosophy, teaching, and learning. Watching Miller lecture on autoimmunity, which he describes ironically as a "light lecture," initiates a tone in the film that perdures. Even when Miller is speaking about death, he radiates a sense of humor that is touching and remarkable. His generosity of spirit is captured here in a myriad of moments that are often subtle and fleeting. The trademark Miller wink is a case in point. Other highlights of the film include Miller's readings of Yeats' "The Cold Heaven," Tennyson's "Tears, Idle Tears," and his discussion on the utility of reading now. Highly recommended as a first sail into Miller's world, the film is both a testament to, in Kujundžić's phrase, one of the most influential thinkers of our time and a beautiful example of what happens when sensitivity, friendship, and passion combine.

Reading for Our Time: Adam Bede and Middlemarch Revisited (Edinburgh: Edinburgh University Press, 2012).

Simultaneously a very recent book and a very old one, *Reading for Our Time* is a patchwork volume of revised essays and book chapters written between 1974 and 2006. In 1982, *Fiction and Repetition* was published after the editors of that volume decided to excise the two opening chapters from the original manuscript: chapters on George Eliot's *Adam Bede* and *Middlemarch*. The current book is a result of Miller's desire to rework those original chapters and combine over 30 years of research on these two novels into a single book. A dense palimpsest of situated acts of reading, the book's four chapters illuminate elements of Eliot's finely crafted realism so easily glossed over in a hasty review. Readers will find here an Eliot every bit as devastatingly perceptive and intellectually astute as Nietzsche, Freud, or Marx. Deftly turning through ironic gradations of Eliot's satiric narrators and relentlessly pursuing the warp and woof of the linguistic eccentricities of those novels, Miller argues that learning how to read well in our time, or better, for our time (for times to come) is much more than an empty pleasure. Reading well, closely, patiently, responsibly and with the subtlety and labor required of us by a novelist like Eliot, argues Miller, can be the most effective way of showing us how to unmask unchecked ideologies in our own time. After decades of rigorous scholarship of these two nineteenth-century novels, and with an audacity of hope that has become the trademark of his unique approach to criticism, Miller's recent volume is both a personal profession of faith and a powerful panegyric for the utility of reading now.

BIBLIOGRAPHY

Aristotle. *Poetics* in *Aristotle's Theory of Poetry and Fine Art, with a Critical Text and Translation of The Poetics* by S. H. Butcher (London: Macmillan, 1932).

Attridge, Derek, ed. *Jacques Derrida: Acts of Literature* (London: Routledge, 1992).

—. *The Singularity of Literature* (London: Routledge, 2004).

—. "Nothing to Declare: J. Hillis Miller and Zero's Paradox" in *Journal of Cultural Research*, vol. 8, no. 2 (April 2004), pp. 115–21.

Auster, Paul. *The New York Trilogy* (London: Faber & Faber, 1992).

Austin, J. L. *How to Do Things With Words*, 2nd edn, eds. J. O. Urmson and Marina Sbisà (Cambridge: Harvard University Press, 1975).

Beckett, Samuel. *Waiting for Godot* (London: Faber & Faber, 1985).

—. *The Unnamable* in *Samuel Beckett: The Grove Centenary Edition*, vol. 2, ed. Paul Auster (New York: Grove, 2006).

Bennington, Geoffrey. "Inter" in *Post-Theory: New Directions in Criticism*, eds. Martin McQuillan, Robin Purves, Graeme Macdonald and Stephen Thomson (Edinburgh: Edinburgh University Press, 2000a).

—. *Interrupting Derrida* (London: Routledge, 2000b).

Caputo, John D. *Deconstruction in a Nutshell: A Conversation with Jacques Derrida* (New York: Fordham University Press, 1996).

—. *The Prayers and Tears of Jacques Derrida: Religion Without Religion* (Bloomington: Indiana University Press, 1997).

Brontë, Charlotte. *Jane Eyre* (London: Penguin, 2003).

Brontë, Emily. *Wuthering Heights* (Hertfordshire: Wordsworth Editions, 1992).

Carroll, Lewis. *Alice's Adventures in Wonderland and Through the Looking-Glass* (London: Bloomsbury, 2003).

Cohen, Barbara and Dragan Kujundžić, ed. *Provocations to Reading: J. Hillis Miller and the Democracy to Come* (New York: Fordham University Press, 2005).

Conrad, Joseph. *Heart of Darkness* (London: Penguin, 1995).

Couch, Sir Arthur Quiller. *The Oxford Book of English Verse 1250–1918* (Oxford: Clarendon Press, 1943).

Currie, Mark. *Postmodern Narrative Theory* (London: Macmillan, 1998).

de Man, Paul. *Allegories of Reading: Figural Language in Rousseau, Nietzsche, Rilke, and Proust* (New Haven: Yale University Press, 1979).

—. *The Resistance to Theory* (Minneapolis: Minnesota University Press, 1986).

Derrida, Jacques. *Writing and Difference*, trans. Alan Bass (Chicago: University of Chicago Press, 1978).

—. *Margins of Philosophy*, trans. Alan Bass (Chicago: University of Chicago Press, 1986a).

—. *Memoires for Paul de Man*, trans. Cecile Lindsay, Jonathan Culler and Eduardo Cadava (New York: Columbia University Press, 1986b).

—. *The Post Card: From Socrates to Freud and Beyond*, trans. Alan Bass (Chicago: University of Chicago Press, 1987).

—. "Aphorism Countertime" in *Acts of Literature*, ed. Derek Attridge (London: Routledge, 1992a).

—. "Passions: 'An Oblique Offering'" in *Derrida: A Critical Reader*, ed. David Wood (Oxford: Blackwell, 1992b).

—. "Circumfession" in *Jacques Derrida*, trans. Geoffrey Bennington (Chicago: University of Chicago Press, 1993).

—. *Points . . . Interviews 1974–1994*, ed. Elizabeth Weber, trans. Peggy Kamuf (Stanford: Stanford University Press, 1995).

—. "The Villanova Roundtable: A Conversation with Jacques Derrida" in *Deconstruction in a Nutshell* by John D. Caputo (New York: Fordham University Press, 1996).

—. *Without Alibi*, trans. Peggy Kamuf (Stanford: Stanford University Press, 2002).

—. "Justices" in *Provocations to Reading: J. Hillis Miller and the Democracy to Come*, eds. Barbara Cohen and Dragan Kujundžić (New York: Fordham University Press, 2005a).

—. *On Touching—Jean-Luc Nancy*, trans. Christine Irizarry (Stanford: Stanford University Press, 2005b).

—. *The Gift of Death*, 2nd edn, trans. David Wills (Chicago: University of Chicago, 2008).

Derrida, Jacques and Maurizio Ferraris. *A Taste for the Secret*, trans. Giacomo Donis, eds. Giacomo Donis and David Webb (Cambridge: Polity, 2002).

Dickens, Charles. *The Pickwick Papers*, ed. Robert L. Patten (London: Penguin, 1982).

—. *David Copperfield*, ed. Trevor Blount (London: Penguin, 1985).

—. *Great Expectations*, ed. Charlotte Mitchell (London: Penguin, 1996).

Eliot, George. *Silas Marner* (London: Macmillan, 1984).

Emerson, Ralph Waldo. *Selections from Ralph Waldo Emerson*, ed. Stephen E. Whicher (Boston: Houghton Mifflin Company, 1960).

Freud, Sigmund. "The Uncanny" in *The Penguin Freud Library Vol. 14: Art and Literature*, trans. James Strachey (London: Penguin, 1985), pp. 335–76.

Hardy, Thomas. *The Mayor of Casterbridge* (London: Penguin, 1997).

—. *Jude the Obscure* (Oxford: Oxford University Press, 1998).

Hemingway, Ernest. "A Clean, Well-Lighted Place" in *The Oxford Book of American Short Stories*, ed. Joyce Carol Oates (Oxford: Oxford University Press, 1992).

Herrick, Robert. *The Poems of Robert Herrick* (Oxford: Oxford University Press, 1920).

James, Henry. *The Art of the Novel: Critical Prefaces* (New York: Charles Scribner's Sons, 1947).

Jeffares, A. Norman. *A Commentary on the Collected Poems of W. B. Yeats* (Stanford: Stanford University Press, 1968).

Johnson, Barbara. *The Critical Difference: Essays in the Contemporary Rhetoric of Reading* (Baltimore: The Johns Hopkins University Press, 1985).

Joyce, James. *Ulysses*, annotated student's edition, ed. Declan Kiberd (London: Penguin, 1992).

Kujundžić, Dragan. (dir.) *The First Sail: J. Hillis Miller* (Deer Isle Productions, 2011).

Lawrence, D. H. *Women in Love* (London: Penguin, 1996).

Lodge, David. *The Novelist at the Crossroads: And Other Essays on Fiction and Criticism* (Ithaca: Cornell, 1971).

McHale, Brian. *Postmodernist Fiction* (London: Routledge, 2001).

Melville, Herman. *Moby-Dick* (New York: Barnes & Noble Books, 1993).

—. *Billy Budd* in *Herman Melville: Tales, Poems, and Other Writings*, ed. John Bryant (New York: The Modern Library, 2001).

Montgomery, R. A. *The Abominable Snowman, Choose Your Own Adventure No.1* (Waitsfield: Chooseco, 2006).

Moynihan, Robert. *A Recent Imagining: Interviews with Harold Bloom, Geoffrey Hartman, J. Hillis Miller, Paul de Man* (Hamden, CT: Archon, 1986).

Nabokov, Vladimir. *Lolita* (London: Weidenfeld and Nicholson, 1960).

Nietzsche, Friedrich. *The Birth of Tragedy*, trans. Shaun Whiteside (London: Penguin, 1993).

Oates, Joyce Carol, ed. *The Oxford Book of American Short Stories* (Oxford: Oxford University Press, 1992).

O'Brien, Flann. *At Swim-Two-Birds* (London: Penguin, 2000).

Pound, Ezra. *ABC of Reading* (New York: New Directions, 1960).

Royle, Nicholas. *Jacques Derrida* (London: Routledge, 2003a).

—. *The Uncanny* (Manchester: Manchester University Press, 2003b).

—. *In Memory of Jacques Derrida* (Edinburgh: Edinburgh University Press, 2009).

Said, Edward. *Beginnings: Intention and Method* (Baltimore: Johns Hopkins, 1978).

Sassoon, Siegfried. "Everyone Sang" in *The Oxford Book of English Verse 1250–1918*, ed. Sir Arthur Quiller-Couch (Oxford: Clarendon Press, 1943a).

—. "In Me, Past, Present, Future Meet" in *The Oxford Book of English Verse 1250–1918*, ed. Sir Arthur Quiller-Couch (Oxford: Clarendon Press, 1943b).

Shakespeare, William. *The Complete Works*, eds. Stanley Wells and Gary Taylor (Oxford: Clarendon Press, 1994).

Stack, George J. *Nietzsche and Emerson: An Elective Affinity* (Athens: Ohio University Press, 1992).

Stevens, Wallace. *The Collected Poems of Wallace Stevens* (New York: Vintage, 1990).

Tennyson, Alfred Lord. *Selected Poems of Tennyson*, ed. Sir John Squire (London: Macmillan, 1959).

Wilde, Oscar. *The Picture of Dorian Gray* (London: Penguin, 1994).

Wolfreys, Julian. *Deconstruction • Derrida* (New York: St. Martin's Press, 1998a).

—. ed. *The Derrida Reader: Writing Performances* (Edinburgh: Edinburgh University Press, 1998b).

—. *Glossalalia—An Alphabet of Critical Keywords* (Edinburgh: Edinburgh University Press, 2003).

—. *Thinking Difference: Critics in Conversation* (New York: Fordham, 2004).

—. ed. *The J. Hillis Miller Reader* (Edinburgh: Edinburgh University Press, 2005).

Yeats, W. B. *The Variorum Edition of the Poems*, eds. Peter Allt and Russell K. Alspach (London: Macmillan, 1966).

INDEX

138 INDEX